How To Learn Anything In Half The Time

BY

CHRISTOPHER W. JONES

YOU ARE TWICE AS SMART AS YOU THINK!
The five simple actions inside this book will prove this to you -
by doubling your reading speed... your power to solve problems...
your ability to completely out think others when you have to!

How To Learn Anything In Half The Time

BY

CHRISTOPHER W. JONES

OLD INC PUBLISHING

Published in Auburn, Alabama by OLD Inc Publishing.

For my parents,
Ray and Rachel Jones

who were always there encouraging me to learn
and who instilled in me the love of reading.

For my wife,
Rebecca

who supported me in my one addiction - books.

For my children,
Alexandra, Ethan, and Isabel

never stop learning.

CONTENTS

PREFACE

This book grew out of a simple idea: That you don't have to be a scholar to learn. That learning – fast, powerful learning of any subject you choose – *can be made easy beyond most people's wildest dreams, if they are only taught a few simple ACTIONS that make facts pop right into their minds!*

Yes – ACTIONS! Not theories. Not principles. Not abstract rules that demand a genius to put them to work.

But simple physical ACTIONS! Things you can do immediately. As simple as picking up a pencil. Opening a book the right way. Copying down problems on a piece of paper so that they half-solve themselves.

These LEARNING ACTIONS were not invented by me. They are the result of years of work by teachers, tutors, authors of speed-learning adult-education courses, management - training executives – everyone, in fact, who has been given the responsibility of making learning easy – and making it fun.

These simple actions – designed for practical people who are pressed for time but realize that they have to learn to forge ahead in life – are collected for the first time in this book. Though there are literally dozens of them in the pages that follow, I have tried to stress the following five – *probably the most profitable five actions you will ever learn in your life!*

1) How to flash-read the printed page. So well that you will eventually be able to pull the core ideas out of many books in about thirty minutes. (See chapters 6 to 8 for the full discussion.)

2) How to develop a Computer-Like Memory for the spoken word. (See chapter 12.)

3) How to build a power-packed vocabulary. (See chapter 4.)

4) How to burn facts, figures, whole books into your memory. (See chapter 20.)

5) How to write simple, clear, compelling English. (See chapters 13 and 14.)

Remember – there is no theory here. Just step by step methods – techniques – ACTIONS that give RESULTS overnight.

This is a book on learning how to learn – not by dreaming but by doing! Let's get on with it –

INTRODUCTON

A SHORT SURVIVAL COURSE FOR THIS RAPID-PACED WORLD IN WHICH WE LIVE

What the ability to learn really means to your future.

Let me be brutally frank right at the start. In this modern, technical, automated world of ours, *your future success or failure is going to depend almost entirely upon your ability to absorb facts, skills and concepts – and put them to immediate use!*

This all-important fact must be repeated over and over again: *No matter what your age – whether you are a man or woman – self-employed or working for a giant corporation – the entire quality of your life will be determined by your ability to learn, to think, to make your mind perform.*

By this I mean that the size of your income, the station you attain in life, the kind of person who will choose you as his friend, even the satisfaction you get out of your sparetime activities – all will be decided by your ability to keep up with the thousands of men and women who are competing with you – and, if possible, forge ahead of them.

Does this sound exaggerated? Then consider these cold, hard facts:

1) About ONE-THIRD of your entire adult life is spent at work. We spend more time at our jobs than we do with our spouse and family. We earn our income from our jobs – gain our status from our jobs – make our friends from our jobs.

2) And yet – from the very first day that you apply for that job – *you are rated acceptable or rejectable on the basis of your ability to absorb facts, to master skills!* For example, if you have a high school diploma, you will earn $150,000 more during your lifetime than if you have only a grade school diploma! And if you have a college diploma, you will earn $250,000 more than that high school graduate!

3) Here is the first rough measurement of what the power to learn is worth in dollars and cents – $250,000 – *a quarter of a million dollars extra for being able to use the God-given power in your brain!* (And this extra income is yours, at any stage of your life – if you learn how to put this brain power to

2

work! You can go out and start on the road to that long-desired degree, *just one short week from today,* when you finish this book!)

4) But the high school diploma, college degrees, professional degrees *are only the start* of the overwhelming impact the ability to learn will have on your career! At every rung of the ladder – every time you're considered for a promotion or a new job – your ability to learn *(and your ability to PROVE that learning in formal tests and interviews)* will make the difference between skyrocketing up, or standing still!

There is no doubt that your ability to master facts will determine your rate of progress on your job, your yearly pay scale, whether you'll be put on special managerial staffs, be given expensive training to prepare you for a better position, break ahead of the field, go forward as fast as you really can. Even whether you'll be forced to retire too early, or take a less demanding job, or continue on to the top as before!

All of it – your own self-confidence, your job advancement in dollars-and-cents success every day of your life – depends overwhelmingly on your ability to master facts, ability to squeeze every ounce of power out of your brain that Nature has built into it.

And you do it – as easily as this –

Is It Really that Hard to Absorb Facts? The Answer Is No.

Once – perhaps ten years ago – the facts I've listed above might have been considered a life sentence of failure for the man or woman who had lost the ability to master facts . . . to absorb the written word . . . to soak knowledge up like a sponge, and put it to work – immediately!

We might have believed this ten years ago. But today we realize that it's a myth.

Again, let's look at the facts.

Given average ability, men and women who have trouble learning in adult life do so because no one had ever taught them to study efficiently when they were children!

Without the proper study techniques, it is perfectly possible for you to understand only HALF what you should get out of a newspaper, magazine, textbook, business letter or report! Without the proper retention techniques, it is possible for you to remember only HALF of what you have just read. And without the proper techniques of filing and retaining that information you have just learned, it is possible for you to put to work only HALF of the

3

knowledge you really have stored away in your brain! We doom ourselves, through our negligence of the proper study techniques, to struggling through life as a HALF-DOER.

You do not have to be brilliant to succeed in life. The only thing separating the average man from a fruitful intellectual life is DIRECTION – the ability to get the best possible results out of your own efforts.

Given this direction, any man or woman with average intelligence can learn new facts almost as quickly as he can read them. Every year, men and women who know how to study obtain business and social success far beyond that which might be expected from their IQ ability level. The difference is TECHNIQUE, pure and simple.

Technique . . . Direction . . . Guidance . . . Method! These are the secrets of success in life. Not an IQ. Not "inborn ability." Not some mysterious hidden talent that enables a few gifted people to solve problems at a glance that other people would never be able to understand, no matter how hard they worked on them.

This idea is pure nonsense. The real difference between the top producer and the mediocre also-ran lies, not in ability, but in technique. And technique can be TAUGHT.

Because of this one simple fact – and because of the almost miraculous breakthroughs that have been achieved in the last few years in teaching people how to learn – there is no longer any reason for any man or woman to be forever catching up while his friends are going forward, to suffer the gloom and discouragement of always being behind, to experience learning as drudgery and disappointment, to be branded as dull or slow-minded, and to be known forever as a four-cylinder mind in an eight-cylinder society.

Learning is a skill, and it can be improved by practice like any other skill.

The ability to learn can be improved drastically by applying a few simple techniques of learning strategically. And YOU can teach yourself enough of these techniques in a single week to literally start yourself on the road to learning anything in half the time.

Here Is Exactly What This Book Will Do For You.

This is the purpose of this book. To teach you how to increase your power to learn with the least effort, in half the time.

What exactly will these techniques do for you you?

Simply this:

1. They will destroy present habits that make learning unpleasant and burdensome, and replace them with new, simpler, and easier habits that turn study into a thrilling, soaring hour of achievement every time you open a book.

2. In other words, they will reduce effective learning procedures to the habit level. They will make them *a part of your mind,* so that you get right down to the core of every lesson, every report, every article – automatically, the instant you set your eyes on it.

3. Because of these new habits, and sooner than you dare expect today, your ability to learn and to perform will zoom, will reveal such a change that your boss or friends may actually ask you what happened.

4. Self-improvement periods – learning periods will shrink in time – sometimes actually in half – while the work turned out from them will double in quantity and quality.

5. And there will be no more forcing yourself to learn. Learning will suddenly become a privilege rather than a punishment, because each new lesson will give you a new taste of success, a new thrill of understanding, a stronger and stronger realization that you can conquer knowledge and make it your own, day after day.

Isn't this worth one week's pleasant reading right now, and a few minutes' thrilling application every day while you're forging ahead?

That's all it takes. All the equipment you need is right here. These simple rules apply to any man or woman, with an average inborn intelligence, with any level of previous education.

To put them to work for YOU – to carve out the life of success and achievement you want for YOURSELF – you start right here.

PART ONE

THE SIMPLE STRATEGY OF POWER LEARNING

CHAPTER 1

HOW GOOD ARE YOUR LEARNING HABITS TODAY? TAKE THIS THREE-MINUTE TEST

Are you living up to your full potential? Are you squeezing out the absolute top achievement that your inborn intelligence will give you?

In other words, are your present learning habits helping or hindering you? Is the power of your brain being harnessed from the very first minute you open a book – or blocked every step of the way?

This three-minute check-list will tell you right now. It is a quick, scientific run-down, not of your intelligence or ability, but of the results your present learning habits are capable of giving you.

Simply observe your learning habits for a single night. Then answer these questions with a yes or a no. In three brief minutes, every weak spot in your learning pattern will be thrown into the spot-light. You'll see the road-blocks in your way, and you'll take your first step toward removing them.

Here they are. Answer them coldly and honestly.

DO YOU:

Find it hard to keep your mind on what you're reading?

Have trouble picking out the main points of the book you're reading?

Forget the next day what you read the night before?

Have trouble finding books, pencils, notes, reports you want to work with?

Take hours to get yourself going on the material you want to learn?

Spend fruitless hours trying to figure out standard problems in business mathematics?

Make the same mistakes over and over again?

Have difficulty expressing your thoughts on paper?

Imitate other people's reports, memos and letters rather than create your own?

Forget new vocabulary words almost as fast as you learn them?

Write letters that are a mess of illegible scribbles and torn-up pages?

HOW GOOD ARE YOUR LEARNING HABITS TODAY?

Never finish work on time?

Cram desperately for advancement tests?

Become sick with fear before such tests?

How many questions did you answer with yes? If there was even one, this book will be worth far more to you than the price you paid for it.

If you had four yes answers, then you are losing over 25 per cent of your brain power through sloppy learning habits. In other words, you are achieving at least 25 per cent poorer results than your inborn ability should give you. This book will restore those lost percentage points.

And if you had eight or more yes answers, then you are in trouble; you can see it at a glance; and you are in for one of the most dramatic and painless improvement performances of your entire life.

Save this test. Check your answers, in pen or pencil, on this page. Refer back to each yes answer – to each weak point – as you reach the section that covers it in this book.

Then, one week from now, when you've finished this book, and you have run through the methods described in its pages – at that point take this test again. Write down your new answers – one week from today – next to the old.

The difference may actually take your breath away. You can actually see yourself grow, see your learning habits change in that first week, see yourself turn the corner to success.

And if there any yes answers left at the end of that first week – then simply mark those weak points. Run over the procedures again. And repeat the test one month later.

You'll see those yes answers evaporate like water on a hot stove. *And you'll see the results of those procedures – in black and white – on your next rating sheet – on the faces of your boss and friends – on the type of people you can now hold spell-bound with your conversation – on the type of book you can now read and repeat – on the new promotion you've earned – the raise you've deserved – the feeling of sheer simple satisfaction you've carved out for yourself – with your own mind!*

CHAPTER 2

OUR PLAN OF ATTACK FOR MORE LEARNING POWER OVERNIGHT – THIS IS ALL YOU HAVE TO DO!

In the past few years, a great many people have become confused. They have become so fascinated with social studies, physics, foreign languages, and the like, that they have forgotten how simple a good education really is.

A good education – a bedrock education – an education upon which you will either succeed or fail for the rest of your life – *consists of just three simple skills:*

The ability to read.

The ability to express thoughts in words, and

The ability to solve mathematical problems.

THE THREE SIMPLE BUILDING BLOCKS OF SUCCESS

Reading, writing and arithmetic. The old-timers knew it. We've forgotten it; and we have to get back to it. These are the foundation stones. Everything else, all the advanced subjects, depends on them. For example, if you can't understand what you read, you can't read science.

If you can't express your own thoughts, you can't write good advertising copy. If you can't solve simple problems in addition or subtraction, then you won't even be able to start on calculus or aerodynamics.

Everything you do in your business life, for example, depends upon your ability to read, to write, and to figure. For the rest of your life, you'll be reading newspapers, memos, articles, and reports. For the rest of your life, you'll be writing letters, applications, recommendations, and progress reports. For the rest of your life, you'll be figuring grocery bills, installment charges, mortgage payments, and profit and loss.

If you can't read like an expert, write like an expert, and figure like an expert, then anything else you do for your mind will be wasted.

Therefore your fundamental task – the one great secret of building success into your life – is to make absolutely sure that you're a "blooming genius" in reading, writing and mathematics.

And I mean genius! When we get through with that mind of yours, we're going to have your friends pop-eyed at your ability to read a printed page, to turn out a written report, to cut through a mathematical problem to its very heart.

Reading, writing, and mathematics. You are going to make yourself a master in each of these. And you are going to do it in five short minutes a day, using these three incredibly powerful tools:

Brand-new scientific techniques.

Daily application.

And that wonderful feeling of accomplishment every time you master something new!

Here's how they combine to get you off to a whiz-bang start – today.

WHAT YOU READ MEANS NOTHING.
IT'S WHAT YOU CAN PUT TO USE THAT COUNTS

Your primary job, then, is twofold. First you must teach yourself the new scientific techniques of reading, writing, and mathematics contained in this book.

And second, you must put them to use, every day, so you can make absolutely sure you've got them right.

This is the one-two punch that knocks tough subjects into a cocked hat, that shoots learning power up overnight.

In computer language, this daily check-up process is called "feedback." Engineers know that it's not what you feed into a computer that counts; it's what that computer does with that information – what it "feeds back" to you – that counts. Some of that information can be lost, forgotten, or distorted. You have to ask for it again to make sure.

The same with your own mind. In everything you learn, for every day of your life, what you read means nothing. Words can simply pour in and out of your mind like water through a funnel. The only thing that counts is what sticks. How much you understand. How much you remember. And how much you can put to immediate use.

Burn this fact into your mind. To learn any subject, mere reading is only the first step. *The complete, effective learning process is made up of these four steps:*

Reading

Understanding

Remembering, and

Reproducing the key thoughts in your own words.

This is the end goal you want. Reproducing, putting to use, expressing in your own words, either on paper or in conversation with your friends. (Or, in the case of mathematics, in solving new problems.)

This is what you are aiming at, the end result. If your learning process stops short of this goal, this effective selfexpression, then you are getting only half the benefit of your work.

You have to make sure that you get it all. You have to apply these incredibly powerful new learning techniques every single day. Here's how you do it:

THE TEN-MINUTE ACHIEVEMENT CHECK ON THE MATERIAL YOU LEARN FROM THIS BOOK

Starting today, and continuing for every day that you read this book, do this:

Spend at least ten minutes a day putting these new ways of learning to work. The time of day is unimportant; but you must be able to give that time completely to your work, in full concentration upon these new methods, with no interruptions and no sense of being hurried.

For these few minutes each day, nothing in the world matters but your mind and the accomplishments it is giving you!

This will be the time you first read a magazine article in five minutes and startle your friends that very same night by rattling off every main point contained in it.

This will be the time you first open the door to a new field of knowledge you've always dreamed of mastering – psychology, law, engineering, computer programming – and find that you can now flash through it – absorbing its facts and theories like a sponge.

Yes, this is the time when you just discover that you can put words on paper that sing – that grasp men's attention – that change their minds – that make them act in the paths and directions that you want them to act!

At the beginning, you will work no more than ten minutes a day. But then, as your skill grows greater and greater – as you become more and more confident in your own ability to learn – you will want to devote more time each day to this thrilling new opportunity for self-expression and self-growth.

You will understand – perhaps for the first time in your life – the true joy of learning!

In summary:

Your entire education rests on your mastery of three bedrock skills:

Reading,

Writing, and

Mathematics.

The purpose of this book is to help you improve those skills to the point of near-perfection. This is done in two ways:

1. By teaching yourself new scientific techniques of learning how to learn; and

2. By checking back on your growth every day, to make sure you have understood these techniques and put them to use.

Through this simple procedure, you will automatically learn a respect for, and a striving toward, that most magic of all words – excellence.

We are striving in this book for excellence. Nothing less will do.

And we begin by teaching you a few simple tricks of organization, to help you get twice as much done in half the time you spend today.

CHAPTER 3

ORGANIZATION – HOW TO GET TWICE AS MUCH DONE IN HALF THE TIME

Most people waste at least half their reading and learning time, because no one has ever shown them how to organize their work.

This is the purpose of this chapter – to cut the waste out of your learning, and make sure you get a full minute's results for every minute you spend with your books.

WHAT IS ORGANIZATION?

Organization is simply *planned direction*. It is a procedure. A system. A planned schedule of events or tasks, one after the other, that gets something done in the shortest possible time, with the least amount of waste.

It is doing the right thing at the right time. And not wasting your time doing the wrong thing.

In regard to your learning-growth, therefore, organization is basically a way of sitting down at a desk,

finding out what has to be done,
opening the right book to the right page,
starting to do it at the beginning,
learning it step by step,
knowing when it is finished and when it is right,
and then remembering what it is you have done, how you have done it,
and what use you can put it to tomorrow.

Without such a definite step-by-step plan of attack, you waste much time. Because you will not get down to work immediately. You will not be sure exactly what it is you are supposed to learn. You will wander aimlessly till you stumble on it. And then you may lose it again, or waste time reading on after you have learned it, or forget it before you get to use it the next day.

Therefore the most beautiful thing about organization is that it is *far simpler and far easier* than what you are doing today. It not only gives you far better understanding – instantly) – but it does it with far less study time.

And it's so easy to put into practice. All the organization you need can be broken down into two simple formulas:

1. Getting down to work; and
2. Doing the work right.

Let's look at each of them in turn.

NO MORE CRISES. NO MORE FEAR

Any subject you wish to learn becomes easy if you organize it on a long-term basis, day by day, lesson by lesson, step by step. Constant, daily study periods, therefore, are the first magic key to success.

The first step in organizing your study habits is to set up a daily work schedule, and make sure you stick to it.

There is just no substitute for regular daily study – for a certain amount of time spent daily on each subject. Learning – any kind of learning – becomes incredibly easy if you maintain a steady pace from start to finish of the subject you want to learn. Then there are no sudden pressures to get things done. No near-hysteria about deadlines. No tensions and anxieties if you're going to take a test to earn a degree in that subject.

With a daily work schedule, religiously enforced, all these crises are miraculously replaced by the wonderfully secure feeling of being adequately prepared. Which, in turn, leads to a steady, comforting flow of high marks towards that degree you may be seeking.

Let's look at such a daily schedule, and see how simple it is to set up, and how easy it is to follow.

YOUR DAILY ACHIEVEMENT SCHEDULE

Monday through Friday

7:00 A.M.	– Get-up time.
7:05 - 7:30	– Wash, dress, shine shoes.
7:30 - 7:45	– Breakfast.
7:45 - 8:00	– Help around the house.
8:00 - 8:10	– Final preparation for work.
8:10 - 8:30	– Going to work.
8:30 - 8:45	– Pre-work talk with friends.
8:45 - 12:45	– Regular work schedule.

12:45 - 1:45   –   Lunch.

1:45 - 5:45   –   Work.

5:45 - 6:05   –   Going home.

6:05 - 7:00   –   Dinner.

6:30 - 6:45   –   Help with clean-up.

6:45 - 7:00   –   *Make ready for study time – get all equipment together.*

7:00 - 8:00   –   *Study hour {or half-hour, or whatever time you prefer).*

8:00 - 11:00   –   Watch TV, read, relax.

11:00 - 11:15   –   Prepare for bed.

11:15 - 7:00   –   Sleep.

Saturday   –   a free day.

Sunday   –   a free day.

The exact details in this schedule are, of course, merely suggestions. Your own family activities may dictate different dinner hours, relaxation breaks, and so on.

But the important points are clear. Every day – every single day – there should be a definite period for learning and application of what you have learned. Without exception. Without excuse. Without delay.

This study period is essential to your career. *And it must start at exactly the same time each night. It must be entered into without delay. And it must be followed by a careful, concentrated check on what you've learned before you can close your books and go on to something else.*

Let's take a closer look at that daily study period and see how we can make it produce twice the results for you.

TIPS THAT DOUBLE THE VALUE OF EACH STUDY HOUR

1. You will not do top work in your study period unless you make that study period as important to you as your work down-town. This means:

2. You must have a definite place to study. It must be the same place each night. With no one else having any claim to it for that hour.

3. It must be comfortable and bright. With the physical equipment you need to read and write permanently stored there, instantly at hand when you want to use it.

4. There must be no distractions for that hour. This means, ideally, a room with the door closed. No Internet, cell phones or TV. No interruptions. No friends working with you. No phone calls permitted for any reason. When you get down to work, you stay at work till you're finished. This means no other members of the family with you. No conversations near by, no rustle of newspapers. You need silence to concentrate. And you have to make whatever sacrifices are necessary to give it to yourself.

5. But this ruling out of distractions goes one step further. It also means that you have with yourself, at study time, only the equipment you need and nothing more. No unnecessary books. No newspapers. No pretty pictures on the wall to draw away your attention. Study is business – all business.

6. Make sure you start your lessons at the same exact moment every day. A five-minute delay can kill an entire study period. The phone conversation is cut off, and you're at your desk at the precise moment you're scheduled to be there.

7. You are setting up a *routine*. A constant, daily psychological readiness to study. An automatic ability to concentrate that can only come from getting down to work at the same time, in the same spot, every day. Once this routine is established, waste motion is eliminated and work flashes by. At the end of that period, when you are ready to review that work, you will be delighted at the quantitiy and quality of it.

In summary:

Organization is planned direction. It is your ability to

1. Cet down to work without waste motion, and

2. Get the work done right.

In this chapter we have seen that organization makes even the hardest subjects easy by attacking them on a day after day basis.

In order to do this, a definite hour must be set aside every day, at exactly the same time, in exactly the same spot, with exactly the same equipment.

Once this routine is established, getting down to work becomes instant and automatic. You're ready to slash into your work without a second's waste motion.

CHAPTER 4

THE SWEET SPOT OF LEARNING

Gnothi Seauton – Know Thyself. These were the words inscribed at the entrance of the Temple of Apollo at Delphi. This is where the quest to learn anything in half the time must begin.

While Rudyard Kipling's Six Honest Serving Men (What, Why, When, How, Where and Who) may have served him, we only need three of them. As explicitly stated in Simon Sinek's book titled "Start With Why" that is where we will begin. We will then proceed to move on to the How and the What. In order to learn anything faster one needs to take a much more active approach to learning verses the traditional passive approach.

So let's take a look at the Why How What methodology. This methodology represents the strategy of learning faster while the rest of the book will cover tactics to help you learn faster.

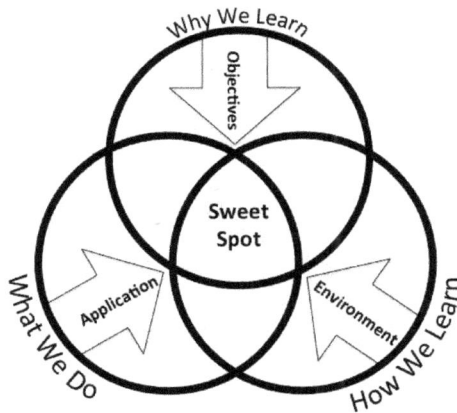

The Why is the reason you are learning – this helps to understand going into it as to what you need to get out of it. Think of Why as the objective of learning. The How is the environment and the media of the learning process

The What is the action you are going to take, want to take or will take after you process the information. One huge key to learning and retention is to apply what you have just learned immediately. This speed of implementation is what sets many successful people apart from us mere mortals.

The intersection of these areas is the sweet spot of learning – very much like the sweet spot on a tennis racket – when you hit this spot everything becomes infinitely more powerful and fluid and you learn faster.

Why

With the rapid and ever increasing rate of change in the world and the amount of information that is available to us it is becoming more and more critical to be able to learn faster and faster. Being able to learn faster is a skillset that will help you in your personal and professional life. Think if this as the overall objective to reading this book. Your big Why!

So why do adults want or need to learn? We have a range of different motivations for selecting a course/program or for learning something. Some of the reasons we may choose to take a course include:

- For personal development purposes, e.g. communication or financial management skills
- For professional advancement, e.g. upgrading of skills to enhance employability or change careers
- To meet employment expectations, e.g. an employer may require that the person attend
- To bring additional skills to the workplace, e.g. presentation skills or information technology skills
- To develop skills which will benefit the local community
- To sample a topic which they might consider studying in greater depth
- To prepare for further study/full-time education
- To resolve personal problems, e.g. conflict resolution
- To facilitate/accommodate life changes, e.g. retirement or parenting
- To make or maintain social relationships
- For escape or stimulation
- For interest only

This is by no means a comprehensive list of why adults learn but hopefully it will give you an idea of what to look for when trying to define you Why. Once you have your Why, write it down in your journal, notebook or even on an index card so that you can keep it with you as you continue with what it is you are learning. With your objective clear, you will now have a laser focus as to what you need to get out of the material and in most cases ignore the fluff.

A friend of mine once told me that my presentations were like a Texas Long Horn. I had a point here, a point way over there and a whole lot of bull in between. By looking specifically for the points here and there, you can ignore the bull in between.

Your Why will also inform your What in that once you know the objective of what you are learning you will then also be able to determine What you will do with the information once you have learned it. Make sure that your Why is a tangible and concrete objective.

How

The next step in the process of learning is to do some self-examination as to how you learn best. There are numerous Learning Styles Inventories available and I do not have time to go into them all so I will just mention a few and leave it up to you to do your own assessment of both the Learning Styles and also your own How.

It has been commonly recognized that each person prefers different learning styles and techniques. Learning styles group common ways that people learn. Everyone has a mix of learning styles. Some people may find that they have a dominant style of learning, with far less use of the other styles. Others may find that they use different styles in different circumstances. There is no right mix. Nor are your styles fixed. You can develop ability in less dominant styles, as well as further develop styles that you already use well.

Using multiple learning styles and multiple intelligences for learning is a relatively new approach. This approach is one that educators have only recently started to recognize. Traditional schooling used (and continues to use) mainly linguistic and logical teaching methods. It also uses a limited range of learning and teaching techniques. Many schools still rely on classroom and book-based teaching, much repetition, and pressured exams for reinforcement and review.

By recognizing and understanding your own learning styles, you can use techniques better suited to you. This improves the speed and quality of your learning.

Stephen Covey said that "Awareness builds its own momentum." By being aware of the different learning styles and by examining your How, you are starting to take a more active role in the learning process which in turn will continue to build momentum.

One of the theories that has developed from recent cognitive research is that of Multiple Intelligences. Howard Gardner of Harvard has identified seven distinct intelligences. Gardner says that these differences "challenge an educational system that assumes that everyone can learn the same materials in the same way and that a uniform, universal measure suffices to test student learning. Indeed, as currently constituted, our educational system is heavily biased toward linguistic modes of instruction and assessment and, to a somewhat lesser degree, toward logical-quantitative modes as well."

These Multiple Intelligences or Seven Learning Styles are as follows:

1. Visual (spatial):You prefer using pictures, images, and spatial understanding.
2. Aural (auditory-musical): You prefer using sound and music.
3. Verbal (linguistic): You prefer using words, both in speech and writing.
4. Physical (kinesthetic): You prefer using your body, hands and sense of touch.
5. Logical (mathematical): You prefer using logic, reasoning and systems.
6. Social (interpersonal): You prefer to learn in groups or with other people.
7. Solitary (intrapersonal): You prefer to work alone and use self-study.

These learning styles have more influence than you may realize. Your preferred styles guide the way you learn. They will determine if you prefer to read something or if you prefer to have it read to you. They also change the way you internally represent experiences, the way you recall information, and even the words you choose.

In addition to the above intelligences there is a popular inventory called the Canfield Learning Styles Inventory developed by Albert A. Canfield in 1979. One of the benefits of the Canfield LSI is that it breaks the learning styles down into three categories: Conditions for Learning, Areas of Interest and Modes of Learning. These can tell you a lot about how you prefer to learn or how you will learn best.

Here is the framework of the Canfield Learning Styles Inventory:

I. Conditions for Learning

1. Peer: Enjoys teamwork and maintains good peer relationships.
2. Organization: Desires clearly organized coursework relevant assignments.
3. Goal Setting: Wants to set own objectives and procedures, may use feed back to modify these.
4. Competition: Needs to compare own accomplishments with those of others.
5. Instructor: Enjoys a mutually friendly, understanding relationship with the instructor.
6. Detail: Desires specific information about assignments, rules, and requirements.
7. Independence: Likes to work independently and determine own study plan.
8. Authority: Likes a disciplined classroom and knowledgeable instructors.

II. Area of Interest

1. Numeric: Prefers to work with numbers and logic.
2. Qualitative: Likes to work with words or language.
3. Inanimate: Likes working with things, as in building, repairing, designing, or operating equipment.
4. People: Likes working with people--interviewing, counseling, selling, or helping.

III. Mode of Learning

1. Listening: Prefers to hear lectures, tapes, or speeches.
2. Reading: Prefers to read books, articles, or bibliographic information.
3. Iconic: Likes to interpret diagrams, movies, pictures, graphs.
4. Direct Experience: Learns by handling or performing, as in shop, field, or laboratory classes.

So by identifying your How, you can determine what is your preferred style of learning. By applying this to each opportunity to learn it will greatly impact your ability to learn faster.

For example if you learn best by listening to something then you can focus on the audio however if you learn best by reading you may want to get a copy or transcription of the presentation or program so that you can read it.

What

The What of our methodology and self examination is the output of your learning. What are you going to do with this information that you have taken in. it can also apply to What you do immediately after taking in the information or finishing up the course/program.

One of the best ways to learn and to grow is to reflect on and evaluate your experiences. You may have heard that experience is the best teacher, but without reflection and evaluation of an experience, it is just an experience. The only way to truly learn and grow from an experience, a book, an article, a talk is to evaluate it by asking what it meant to us, what can we learn from it, what can we apply in our lives, what do we need to quit doing based on the experience.

How many times have we read a great book, heard a great talk or had a great experience and thought how much it would help us but never did anything with the information and experience?

Some time ago, I was taught to use the acronym ACT to reflect on teachings and experiences. First I annotate the book or my notes with an A for those things I want to apply in my life. I put a C next to those things I want to change in my life and a T next to those items that I want to transfer or teach to someone else to help them. When I review my notes, I can incorporate these items I have annotated on my calendar or action plan for the week or month. This helps me to make better use of these learning and growth opportunities and keeps me from just taking in useless data.

Here's the final point of this chapter:

"Implement as quickly as you can!"

Ask yourself, how many times in your life you had a "great idea" or a "great opportunity", but you didn't really follow through. Instead you switched yourself into "research mode". Or in "waiting mode" and never switched to "taking action". Later you simply dropped the idea. Another, "what would have been, if this had worked …" story is born. Think a little:

What is research, reading, waiting, … worth?

It's worth exactly 0.00 in any currency.
Unless you put it to work.

The sooner you act, the sooner you put the information or your idea into action, the sooner you'll get results. Positive and sometimes negative ones. The important part is you get solid results that help you stir your business ship into the right direction.

"Thinking about it", "doing research", "reading", "waiting" will not give you the answers you need to boost your life or your business with success stories.

You have to act! Do it now, don't wait. Get into the habit of A.C.T.ing on any new information immediately. A recent university study in the US has revealed again:

The number 1 key factor of successful people is:

"Speed of Implementation"

Now let's go on to the second part of organization: How to fill up that period with achievement. How to do that work right.

We'll start with the basic art of reading. How to cut through it in half your present time, with absolute understanding of every word you read.

PART TWO

DIGGING OUT THE FACTS – READING

CHAPTER 5

THE SHORTCUT WAY TO WORD POWER –
RIGHT DOWN TO RECOGNIZING A NEW WORD
WITHOUT NEEDING A DICTIONARY

The first requirement to be a good reader is *mastery of words.*

As you read, as you listen, as you gain information from any source whatever, you learn new words.

This word-learning is one of the most important parts of your education. *For words are the tools of thought. Mental tools that make thought far easier, far more exact, far more powerful in solving the problems you encounter in your everyday life.*

The more words you leam, the more mental tools you have to work with. The purpose of this chapter is to show you how to master these tools.

HOW TO MAKE YOUR CONVERSATION SPARKLE –
WITHOUT LEARNING A SINGLE NEW WORD!

Let's try a quick word game right now – that you can practice in just two minutes a day – anywhere – without the slightest training in vocabulary building. A word game that will pull out hundreds of Power-Packed words from your "Hidden Vocabulary," and put them to work for you – at once! Let's call this simple exercise the Change-the-Word Game – a search for substitute words in your conversation, and see what magic changes you can make when you fit them in.

For example, take the magnificent line from the Old Testament: "When they were in the field, Cain rose up against Abel and slew him." What would happen if we changed the key words in this sentence? Would we make the sentence better? Would we add or subtract meaning? Ask yourself to try it and see.

Perhaps you will replace "rose up" with such words as *conspired against, blindly hated, treacherously attacked.*

Perhaps you will replace "slew" with such words as *killed, murdered, butchered, assassinated.*

Which of these new words is the most exciting? Which carries the thought best?

As you play on, you learn to search for exactly the right word to project the color and meaning of what you want to say. You feel at home with all kinds of words – small and large, simple and exotic. You add drama and depth to everything you say or write. And you see the difference almost immediately in the way people stop and listen to you – and you alone – when you begin to speak.

Try it for a week. Promise yourself you'll never use "nice," "pretty," "exciting," "good," or other such tired words or phrases again.

Search for emotion-packed, color-packed new words – new ways to express your thoughts – your feelings – your desires. This one simple exercise alone can make a vast difference on the effect your words can have on everyone around you, and it's only the beginning.

HOW TO TEACH YOURSELF TO IDENTIFY
STRANGE WORDS, WITHOUT LOOKING THEM UP

Now you are ready to play the most thrilling and profitable game of all – learning how words are built. Recognizing the meaning of new words without having to interrupt your reading to look them up.

This also can be made an adventure in learning, if you follow this simple, two-step plan:

First of all, you have to realize that all words are built up, part by part, just as a model airplane is.

Words, however, are much more simple. They have just these three basic parts:

1. They have a *roof or stem,* which tells us the basic meaning, such as "go."

2. Then there is the *front part or prefix*, which adds another meaning to the root word, such as "out" plus "go" equals "outgo."

3. And then there is the *end part or suffix,* which gives us still another meaning. For example, "ing," which rounds out our word to give us "out" plus "go" plus "ing" to add up to "outgoing."

Thus we can build one big word out of three small ones. And this gives us a brand-new word, which is much easier to remember, takes far less space to write, and actually gives us a brand-new meaning that we wouldn't have had with the three smaller words at all.

This is the way language grows. By taking two or three small words, and building a new word out of them. And, by doing it, giving us new meanings to solve new problems.

There are three basic building blocks, then, to build new words – the *root*, the *front part,* and the *end part.*

Some words have only the root, like *hear.* Other words have only the root and the end part, like *hearing.* Still others have only the root and a front part, like unheard. And still others have all three parts, like unhearing.

Now, how does this knowledge help you recognize strange words without looking them up? In a very simple way:

Most big words that you don't recognize are actually made up of smaller words, in exactly the manner we have just described. They are made up of the same three basic building blocks we've just examined.

However, most of these smaller word parts are in Latin, for the very simple reason that Latin was the ancient language that was the parent of our own English language.

Therefore, in order to work out the meaning of a strange word the first time you see it, all you have to do is learn these Latin word parts, and see how they fit together to make new words.

THE MOST PROFITABLE WORD GAME YOU WILL EVER PLAY

Listed below are some of the most common Latin and Greek word parts in our language. It has been said that from a mere twelve of these parts, we have built over 2,500 English words. No wonder it pays you such incredible dividends to learn one or two of them every night.

Let's start with the most common front parts. Here's the front part itself, what it means, and a common English word that uses it. Notice how easy the word is to understand at a glance, once you know the meaning of the front part.

FRONT PART	MEANING	COMMON WORD
a, au	not, without	atypical
ab, abs	to free from	absolve
ad	to	adhere
am, amb, ambi	about, around, both	ambiguous
amphi	both, around	amphibious
ante	before	anteroom
ant, anth, anti	opposed to	anti-labor

FRONT PART	MEANING	COMMON WORD
arch, archi	chief, principal	archbishop
aut, auth, auto	self	automatic
bi, bis	two, double	biennial
caco	bad, ill	cacophonous
cata	down, complete	catalogue
circum	around	circumference
cis	on this side of	cisatlantic
col, com, con, cor	jointly	combine
contra, centro	against	contradict
counter	in opposition to	counteract
de	from, down,	
completely	deduce	
di, dis	away from	dismiss
dia	between	dialogue
en	in, into	energetic
ep, eph, epi	upon, on, over	epitaph
equi	equal	equidistant
eu	well, good	euphony
ex, e	out	exit
extra	beyond, outside of	extraordinary
hetero	another, different	heterogeneous
hyper	over	hypercritical
hypo	under, below	hypodermic
i, il, im, in, ir, ig	not	inept
inter	between	interstate
intra	within	intrastate
intro	place before	introduce
mal, male	bad	malpractice
meta	after, change	metaphor
mis	wrong	mislabel
miso	hatred of	misogyny
mono	one, alone	monologue
multi	many	multiply
neo	new	neophyte
non	not	nonsense
ob	against	obstruct
ortho	correct, right	orthoptic
pan	all	panacea
para	beside	parallel

FRONT PART	MEANING	COMMON WORD
per	through	permit
peri	around	perimeter
poly	many	polygon
post	after	postscript
pre	before	prejudge
pro	before	pronoun
proto	first	protocol
pseudo	false, fictitious	pseudopod
psycho	relating to mind or soul	psychology
re, red	back, again	reincarnation
retro	back, backward	retrospect
se, sed	away, aside, apart	secede
semi	half	semi-circle
sub	under	submarine
super	above	superabundant
syn, sy	together	syntax
trans, tra	through, across	transport
tri	three	triangle
ultra	excessive	ultra-modest
un, uni	one	uniform
vice	in place of	vice versa

Now for END PARTS. Notice how they, too, add to the meaning of every word they touch.

END PART	MEANING	COMMON WORD
able, ible	above to be	believable
age	state	marriage
al	belonging to	constitutional
an, ave	belonging to	Georgian
an, ain	a member of	Republican
anee	quality	tolerance
ancy, ency	quality or state of	clemency
ant, ent	one who does	servant
ar	relating to	angular
ard, art	one who does	coward
ary	engaged in	secretary
ate	to make	animate
ation	the act of	dedication
cy	practice of	democracy
dom	state of	martydom

END PART	MEANING	COMMON WORD
ee	one who receives	assignee
eer	one who is engaged in	volunteer
en	to make	moisten
em	belonging to	western
er	one who does	miner
er	belonging	Marylander
ery	occupation	surgery
esque	like, style of	statuesque
ferous	bearing, giving	auriferous
fold	number	twofold
ful	full of	resentful
gram	a writing	telegram
graph	a writing	autograph
hood	state of	brotherhood
ial	pertaining to	editorial
ic, ical	resembling	fantastic
ice	act, quality	justice
ify	to make	gratify
il, ile	capable of being	versatile
ine	of the nature of	canine
ion	the act of	decision
ious	full of	ambitious
ish	characteristic of	bookish
ism	state of	fascism
ist	one who practices	communist
ity	quality of	acidity
ive	tending to	abusive
ize	to follow an action	economize
less	lacking	useless
ling, long	showing direction	headlong
logy	science of	theology
iy	having qualities of	friendly
ment	act or process of	investment
ness	a quality	happiness
ogy	study of	geology
or	one who does	tailor

END PART	MEANING	COMMON WORD
ory	of	prohibitory
ose	containing	verbose
ous	full of	mountainous
ry	practice of	dentistry
sion	the act of	ascension
tion	the act of	inspection
trix	feminine agent	executrix
tude	state of	rectitude
ty	practice of	fidelity
ure	act of	rapture
vorous	feeding on	carnivorous
ward	direction of	eastward
wise	way of	clockwise
wright	maker	playwright
y, ey	pertaining to	smoky

Now the root words themselves. There are, of course, hundreds of them. All we can do is list some of the most common here. If you wish to learn more of them, you can easily find them in any good book on word building.

Again, notice how seemingly hard words become a cinch to understand when you recognize their word parts. And also notice how the front and end parts also build up the meaning of each word.

ROOT WORD	MEANING	COMMON WORD
acer, acr	sharp	acerbity
ag, act, ig	carry on	agency
ali	nourish	alimentary
ali, alio, alle	other	alias
alter	another	alter
alt	high	altitude
ambul	walk	amble
am, em	friend	amicable
amo, ama	love	amorous
anim	life	animation

ROOT WORD	MEANING	COMMON WORD
annu, enni	year	annual
anthrop	man	anthropology
appe	a call upon	appeal
aqua, aque	water	aquatic
arbiter	a judge	arbitration
art	art	artistic
ast, astr	star	astrology
audi, aur, aus	hear	audible
bell	hostile	rebellious
bible	book	bibliography
bio	life	biology
brevi	short	abbreviate
cad, cas, cid	fall	cadence
cam, chamb	room	chamber
camp, champ	country	campus
cant, chant, cent	sing	cantate
ced, ceed, cess	go	recede
celer	speed	accelerate
cent	hundred	century
chief, cap	head	captain
cap, capt	take, seize	capture
chrom, chromo, chroma	color	panchromatic
chron, chrono	time	synchronize
cide, eis, eise	cut, kill	suicide, scissor
cit	arouse	excite
civ, jcivi	citizen	civic
clam, claim	shout	clamor
clud, cluse	close, shut off	exclude
cline	bend	recline
coc, coct	cook	concoct
col, cul	till	cultivate
cor, cord	hear	accord
corp, corps, corpor	body	corporation
cras	tomorrow	procrastinate
cred, creed	believe	incredible

ROOT WORD	MEANING	COMMON WORD
crea	create	creation
cresc, crue, cret, crete	grow	increase
crux, cruc	a cross	crucifix
crypt	hide	cryptogram
culp	guilt	culpable
cur, course	to run	concurrent
cur, cura	care	curate
cycl	wheel	cycle
deca, deci	ten	decade
dem, demo	people	democracy
dens	thick	dense
derm	skin	epidennis
dexter	right-handed	dexterity
di, dia	day	diary
die, diet	speak	dictate
dign	worthy	dignitary
doc, doct	teach	doctrine
dom	master	dominate
dom	house	domestic
dorm	sleep	dormitory
du	two	duet
dur	hard, lasting	durable
duc, duct	lead	educate
dynam	power	dynamic
err	wander, go astray	errant
erg	work	energy
ego	I	egotist
fac	do	factory
fer	carry	transfer
ferv	boil	fervent
fid	faith, trust	fidelity
fil	son	filiate
fin	limit	final
firm	strengthen	affirm
flex, fleet	bend	flexible
flu, flux	flow	fluent

ROOT WORD	MEANING	COMMON WORD
fort	strong	fortress
found, fuse, fund	pour	refund
fract, frang	break	fragile
frater	brother	fraternity
fug	flee	fugitive
gam	marriage	bigamist
go	earth	geography
gen	birth	gender
gest, ger	carry, bear	gestation
gov, gub	govern, rule	government
grad, gress	walk, go	progress
grand	great	grandeur
graph	write	autograph
grat	pleasing, agreeable	gratitude
grav	heavy	gravity
greg	crowd	congregate
hab, hib	have, hold	habit
homos	same	homonym
hydr	water	hydrant
ject	throw	reject
jud	right	judgment
junct, jug	join	junction
juven	young	juvenile
labor	toil, work	laboratory
laud	praise	laudatory
lav	wash, clean	lavatory
leg, lig, lect	read, choose	legible
leg	law	legislature
lib	book	library
liber	free	liberty
H	bind	oblige
liter	letter	literal
loc	place	location
locu, loqu	speak, talk	elocution
log	word	dialogue
lue, lum	light	illuminate
lud, lus	play	allude

ROOT WORD	MEANING	COMMON WORD
magn	great	magnify
mand	order	mandate
man, manu	hand	manual
mar, mari	sea	maritime
mater, matr	mother	maternal
matur	ripe	mature
med	middle	median
men, ment	mind	demented
mens, mest	month	semester
merg	dip	submerge
meter	measure	diameter
mis, mit	send	permit
mon	advise	admonish
morph	shape	amorphous
mor, mort	death	mortal
mov, mot, mob	move	remove
mut	change	mutant
nasc, nat	bom	nativity
nihil	nothing	annihilate
nom, nomin	name	nominate
nov	new	novice
nym	name	pseudonym
oper, opus	work	operator
path	feeling	sympathy
pater, patr	father	paternal
pari	talk	parliament
pars, part	a part	partner
ped, pod	foot	pedal
pel, puis	drive	impulse
pend, pens	hang, weigh	impending
pet	seek, ask	petition
pet, petr	rock	petrify
omni	all	omnibus
phil	love	philosophy
phobia	fear	hydrophobia
phon	sound	telephone
plie	twist	complicate

ROOT WORD	MEANING	COMMON WORD
poli	city, state	political
port	carry	portable
pon, pos	put, place	exponent
pot	power	potentate
prim	first	primary
pris, prehen	seize, grasp	apprehend
prob	test	probation
put	think	compute
pyr	fire	pyromaniac
rog	question	interrogation
reg, rec	direct	direct
rupt	break	rupture
sei, scio	know	conscience
scop	watch	telescope
scrib, script	write	describe
seg, sect	cut	section
sed, ses, sid	seat	session
sens, sent	feel	sentiment
sequ, secu, sue	follow	sequence
sign	sign, mark	designate
sol	alone	solitude
solv, solu	loosen, free	absolve
somin	sleep	insomnia
soph	wise, wisdom	sophomore
spec, spect, spic	look, see	spectacle
spir, spirit	breathe	aspire
spend	promise	despond
sta, sti, sist	stand	circumstance
stead	place	steadfast
strict	bind	district
stru	build	stiucture
tact, ting	touch	tactile
tail	cut	crutail
tang	touch	tangible
tend	extend	extend
tena, tain	hold	detain
tent, tempt	try	attempt

ROOT WORD	MEANING	COMMON WORD
term	end, limit	terminal
terr, ter	earth	inter
tele	afar	telescope
theo	God	Theology
therm	heat	thermometer
thesis	setting, statement	thesis
tor, tort	twist	distort
tract	draw	tractor
trib	pay, grant	tribute
typ	model	typical
umbr	shadow	umbrella
urb	city	urban
val	strength	validity
ven, vent	come	convene
ver	true	veracity
vert, vers, verse	turn	divert
via, voy, vio	way	convey
vine, vict	conquer	victor
vir	man	virile
voc	call	vocation
vol	wish	voluntary
volu, volv, volt	tum, roll	involve
zoo	animal	zoology

And, of course, many more. You should have a page in the back of your notebook. Every time you discover a new word part, and learn its meaning, you should immediately write it down on this page for permanent reference. And, at the same time, you should immediately see how many different words you can find that use this part to build their meaning. This is easily one of the most fascinating and profitable word games you will ever play.

TWO DICTIONARIES EVERYONE SHOULD OWN

To look up these word parts, and to give you the meaning of every new word you might come across in your home studies, you should have your own dictionary. This should be a college dictionary. It will be one of the most-used books in your entire library.

In addition to this personally owned reference dictionary, you should build up a special technical dictionary for every course you study. In every new course, you will have to master the *fundamental vocabulary* for that course.

For example, if you want to improve your grammar, you will have to know the meaning of *noun, pronoun, verb, adjective, adverb, preposition, participle, gerund, declension,* and dozens more.

Special words like these are often defined only once in a textbook – the first time they are introduced – and then are used over and over again throughout the textbook without being defined again. Often you will forget their meaning in the interval, and find that you are hopelessly lost in an advanced lesson.

This can easily be avoided by setting up a Vocabulary Page in the back section of a notebook or your journal.

Here, each time you encounter a new word, you simply write it down on this page, along with its precise definition. Then, when you come across it again in your reading, you can simply look it up on your Vocabulary Page without loss of time or motion.

Remember, you cannot understand a lesson unless you completely understand the meaning of every word in that lesson.

Therefore it's up to you to make sure that you master each one of those words. Go over your Vocabulary Page every night. Make sure you know how to spell it; how to pronounce it; how to use it in a sentence; and how to define it in the shortest possible number of words. Only then do you have that word firmly fixed in your mind, ready to go to work for you on the reading you're going to do tomorrow.

In summary:

Words are incredibly powerful mental tools that help you solve your problems. It has been found that the more successful the man, the larger his vocabulary. Therefore you must master the words you need for success.

This can be easily done, in these three ways:

1. By developing the habit of searching for the exact right word. This enlarges your vocabulary, and gives color and power to every sentence you speak or write.

2. By teaching yourself the Latin and Greek word parts that make up our modem English language, and thus recognize hundreds of strange new words at a glance, without having to interrupt your reading to look them up immediately in a dictionary.

3. By building your own personal Fundamental Vocabulary Dictionary for every course you study. Thus you will gain a complete mastery of the language of that course, gain a deeper understanding of its way of thought, and cut hours of study time from the effort it takes you to master it. We now put these newly learned words to use in your reading and writing. We begin with your reading.

CHAPTER 6

HOW TO BECOME A MASTER READER
IN THREE EASY STEPS

The basic, fundamental skill required for all education is reading.

Your ability to learn effectively, to thoroughly understand any subject, depends almost entirely on your ability to read. On your ability to pull facts out of a printed page and make them your own.

Even in mathematics, you must first read the instructions and then understand precisely what you are to do to solve each of the problems.

If you cannot do this, if you cannot read any printed page that is handed to you with complete confidence and understanding, then you will go through the rest of your life suffering from these two crippling handicaps:

1. You will be forever doing unnecessary work. Every assignment will become doubly difficult – read over and over again two or more times, with each sentence painfully spelled out and only partially understood. And

2. You will be forever making unnecessary mistakes. For example, professional educators acknowledge that almost as many errors are made in tests *through sheer misread ing or misunderstanding of instructions alone as through lack of knowledge.*

Why burden yourself for the rest of your life with this double waste? Especially when effective reading – active, aggressive reading that tears knowledge out of the printed page and burns it into your memory for good – is far easier and far faster than the "spell-along" reading most people do today.

Here's why.

GOOD READING IS FAR MORE THAN MERELY
RECOGNIZING WORDS

We will assume in this book that you already read normally. In other words, that you can take the letters c-a-t and put them together to form the word "cat." And that you can take several such words, and read them in the sentence, "The cat chases the mouse."

This, really, is what most people usually mean when they speak of the activity "reading." That you can mechanically scan a printed page and put the words together from that page to form sentences. In turn, this mechanical reading, by some magic process, is supposed to put knowledge in your mind. According to this theory, once you have read a sentence, or a series of sentences, the thought contained in them is supposed to automatically be transferred into your memory.

This is nonsense. Absolute nonsense. Everyone, at one time or another, has read an entire page, and then not been able to remember a single fact from it five minutes later.

Mere mechanical reading is not enough. Passive reading is not enough. The ability to run your eye over a printed page-to make words out of the print on that page and put them together into sentences – *is only the beginning of Effective Reading.*

Effective Reading is far more than this.

Effective Reading goes one step beyond mere words.

Effective Reading is the art of taking those words, and boiling them down into THOUGHTS. Of bailing down dozens, and even hundreds, of those words into ONE VITAL THOUGHT.

Of searching for the "guts" of an assignment-the two or three really important thoughts that it contains-and separating them from all the waste words and unnecessary details that surround them.

And then burning those few vital thoughts into your memory, so you can never forget them.

GOOD READING IS A SEARCH. A SEARCH FOR BIG IDEAS.

Let me repeat these all-important facts. You must be trained, not merely to read for words, but for *central thoughts.*

You must be taught that good reading is an active, aggressive search that has these three steps:

1. Locating a main idea in the mass of words that contain it.

2. Separating that idea from its unnecessary details. And

3. Boiling that idea down into a few easily remembered words.

You become a good reader, therefore, only when you master this technique of searching and boiling down. Searching and boiling down. Searching and boiling down.

Until you have taken the entire assignment – hundreds upon hundreds of words, sentences, and paragraphs – and reduced them to a few vital thoughts that contain the mean ing of them all, that sum up the meaning of them all. And that can be burned into your memory forever in a few short moments. Ready to be put to use – to solve new problems at business, or to answer questions in an examination – the very instant you need them.

THIS IS A NEW WAY TO READ. TWICE AS FAST. FIVE TIMES AS EFFECTIVE.

The rest of this section will be devoted to teaching you to read this new way. It is surprisingly easy to learn. And it is far easier, and far faster, than your present method.

Let me outline right now what each of the following chapters is going to teach you.

There are three easy steps to this new reading process. Each of the next three chapters explains one of them.

Chapter 6 shows you how to set up the search for big ideas. How to glance over your assignment, in one or two short minutes, and locate each of its important thoughts, *before* you begin to read.

Chapter 7 shows you how to Power-Read. How to flash through page after page, pulling out and marking down those important thoughts, merely glancing over their unnecessary details, and finishing with the assignment in half the time it has taken you before.

Chapter 8 shows you how to boil these vital thoughts down into a few words, and burn them into your memory with the very same action.

And Chapter 9 shows you how to use the same threestep technique when you are listening to a lecture. It enables you to understand and remember what you *hear* as well as what you *read*.

When you have finished this section, and put its simple methods to use, you will be confident, accomplished reader. You will be able to read any book, any article, any letter, any report that is given to you, easily, swiftly, and without fear. You will understand each word you read the instant you read it. And you will remember the vital paints of everything you read and be able to put them to immediate use.

In summary:

Good reading is far more than merely recognizing the meaning of words.

Good reading is an active, aggressive search for the major thoughts that are contained in these words.

This search has three steps:

1. Locating the main ideas.

2. Separating them from their unnecessary details.

3. Boiling them down into a few words that can be easily memorized.

Now let's put these three steps into action. Let's examine each of these techniques in detail, along with concrete examples of what they will accomplish for you.

CHAPTER 7

HOW TO PRE·READ A LESSON -
UNDERSTAND IT BEFORE YOU READ

Let us suppose that you are given a reading assignment in a night schooL For example, you are told to read Chapter 6 in a history book on the Civil War. Or the next five pages in a book on Cost Accounting. Or perhaps even a complete book- let's say *The Red Badge of Courage* by Stephen Crane.

You take the book home. You sit down at your desk at the exact moment your evening study hour begins. And you open the book to the page assigned.

What do you do now?

If you simply begin to read the first words you see - if you plunge right into that text without making any further preparation- then you are making a crucial mistake that will cost you hours of wasted effort every week, and that may cause you to miss the entire point of each lesson.

No one- no matter how bright--can really understand an assignment by simply beginning to read it word after word. It's like trying to go on a car trip by simply driving on to the first highway you see, without getting directions or looking at a road map.

Your job in reading is to get those directions. To build yourself that road map. To know exactly what you want to get out of that lesson. And where it's located.

To do this, you pre·read that lesson. You glance over that lesson from beginning to end-before you start to read it. And you pick out the following information:

1. What's the main theme of this lesson? (For example, the Civil War.)

2. How much information does this lesson cover? (The period from 1861 to 1864.)

3. What are the main thoughts in this lesson that I have to remember? (The crucial battles that turned the tide of the war.)

4. How many of these main thoughts are there? (About five or six.)

5. What do I have to remember about each one of these main thoughts? (The outcome of each battle.)

6. Where in the lesson do I find this information? (Now you begin to read.)

JUST LOOK AT THE DIFFERENCE THESE FEW QUESTIONS MAKE.

Now, what exactly has happened here? You have in vested one or two brief minutes to glance over your lesson from beginning to end. In that short time, you have picked out its main theme and each of its central thoughts. You have built a skeleton of that lesson – an outline of that lesson – a road map of that lesson to follow as you read.

Now you know what you are looking for. Now you are walking a lighted path instead of stumbling in the dark. Now, instead of facing a confused jumble of words, you slash through that lesson with this definite purpose in mind:

What do I have to remember about each one of my main thoughts? (What was the outcome of each battle in this history lesson?)

Now you read to answer this question. You have direction. In one or two minutes, you have a better grasp of that assignment than if you read it aimlessly for a full hour.

HOW YOU FIND THESE MAIN THOUGHTS: SIGNPOSTS IN THE LESSON THAT POINT THEM RIGHT OUT TO YOU

Fortunately, the authors of your books agree with this road-map idea. They too believe that you should first build an outline of the important thoughts in each lesson, and then simply fill in the details.

In order to help you do this, they have built into their books certain signposts that point out these main thoughts. These signposts stick out from the main body of the text.

They are the chapter headings, section headings, table of contents, summary paragraphs, and all other vital points set off by capital letters, underlining, italics, and other attention-drawing devices.

They form a book within a book. And by learning how to read them, you can pick out the main points of that book almost as fast as you can turn its pages.

Let's see how to really use them, right now. Let's start with the big signposts, the ones that will give you the guts of that entire book in five to ten minutes.

And then let's work our way down to the smaller signposts, the ones that will organize your learning each time you read another chapter in that book.

For our first few chapters, we'll use this book - the one you're reading now. This will give you a chance to check your present reading habits, to see if you're getting as much information out of each page as you should.

Then we'll go on to examples from standard textbooks. And then we'll see how the same simple techniques apply to everything you read-let you pull information out of newspapers, magazines, and so on, almost as fast as you can run your eyes down their pages.

Here we go!

SIGNPOST PARTS OF EVERY BOOK
AND WHAT EACH ONE TELLS YOU

1. THE TITLE

What it tells you: Actually, a good title should give you, in a single phrase, the main theme of the book. What it is about, and what it is not about. It is your first concrete information about what you are to learn in the pages that follow. Make sure you understand it before you read on.

Example: The title of this book is *How to Learn Anything in Half the Time.* Here is a deliberately long title, containing two separate pieces of information. First, the subject, which is your ability to learn. Second, a specific goal – to do that in half the time.

Starting from this title, and knowing exactly what you should get out of this book, you read on with one purpose – *to answer the question "how?"*.

How do I learn in half the time?

To answer this question, you turn to the next big signpost part of the book:

2. THE TABLE OF CONTENTS

What it tells you: The table of contents takes the grand plan, the ultimate goal you are shooting for, and breaks it down into a step-by-step process. It shows you the steps you have to take, one after another, to attain that goal.

This table of contents is actually a ready-made outline of the book that should be studied carefully before you read one word of its text. By carefully going over this table of contents, you immediately

gain an over-all picture of the skeleton of the book;

see the relationships between each of the various chapters and the main theme of the book;

know exactly where you are going when you start to read – to such a degree that you can even set up a time schedule of so many days per chapter to finish the book when you have to.

For example: In this book, the table of contents is broken down into six main parts, and then into twenty-four chapters.

Let's start with the main parts first, and see how they give us the over-all plan of the book at a glance. Here they are:

> *The Simple Strategy of Power Learning.* (What we are going to do and how we are going to do it.)
>
> *Digging Out the Facts – Reading.*
>
> *Expressing the Facts – Writing and Conversing.*
>
> *Mastering Facts – The Art of Remembering and Review.*
>
> *High Tech Hacking of the Learning Process.*

By simply glancing at these five titles, you immediately see that the book is going to concentrate on reading, writing, and remembering to the extent of devoting full sections to each of them.

Thus the general goal of learning anything in half the time, which was promised in the title, has now been broken down into specific, step-by-step goals of improving your reading, writing, and ability to solve problems, helping you over problem areas, and sharpening your ability to take tests.

Now the table of contents goes on to show us more concretely how we're going to accomplish each one of these major goals. It does this by listing the chapter headings under each of them. For example, in the next part of this book, on writing, we find these two chapters:

> *Correct Spelling Made Easy.*
>
> *How to Write as Easily and Quickly As You Think.*

Now you can see that there are only two steps to improve your writing. First, spelling; then the actual construction of sentences and paragraphs.

Again we see the grand plan of the book developing before our eyes. From the over-all goal of doubling your power to learn, we have gone on to the six major steps for doing this, and then we have taken one of those steps, which is writing, and learned two separate ways in which it alone can be improved.

We can do the same thing for each of the other four major parts of the book. Each major part of the book has its own chapter headings underneath it, which show you step by step how you are going to achieve it.

You have now finished reading the title and the table of contents. You have spent perhaps five minutes on the book so far. And yet you now know:

1. What it is going to do for you, and

2. How it is going to do it, perfecdy.

From this point on, you will read simply to answer the questions each one of these chapter headings has raised in your mind. For example, going back to the section on writing again:

How do I spell a word correctly when I have misspelled it every time before now?

What are the techniques that allow me to write easily and quickly?

At this point you could open to the first page of text, and read faster and with much greater understanding than you have ever read before.

But, before you do this, there are two other big sign posts you will want to check, to help you get every ounce of information out of that book.

3. THE INDEX.

What it tells you: The index is a storehouse of minor topics of special interest to you. There they are alphabetically arranged for instant reference.

For example: Glance at the index of this book. Pick out a topic of special interest to you, or a problem that you are facing today. For instance, take problem-solving. Look up *problem-solving* in the index. Turn to the pages indicated there. And *glance at, do not read,* the treatment given to them.

Instantly you can see the concrete, step-by-step methods that make those problems easy. There's no need to read them, word by word, now, since you'll get up to them later this week. And in the proper time and place in the book, they'll mean far more to you.

But now you know that they're there, and that they're complete. And if you ever have to refer back to them after you finish the book, the index will tell you where they're located at a glance.

And now we turn to the last of our big signposts:

4. THE INTRODUCTION, OR PREFACE, OR FOREWORD.

What it tells you: This is the author's personal message to you, before he gets down to the body of the book.

In it, he may

> explain why he chose this particular title,

> or tell you what compelled him to write the book,

> or show you in advance what he is trying to accomplish,

> or give you a brief, one or two paragraph condensation of its contents,

> or list the main sources from which he got his information, or list the reasons why this book should be important to you,

> or in any other way give you a brief outline of where you will be heading in the book and what benefits it will give you.

It is the personal note, the personal touch that rounds out your quick survey of the book and gives you insight into the author himself and his purpose in writing the book, as well as its contents.

For example: The introduction in this book is divided into three distinct parts, each of which serves a very definite purpose.

Part 1 of the introduction points out the overwhelming importance of learning power to your future, and lists ten reasons why it is so vital.

Part 2 shows you that this door-opening ability to absorb and use facts is really not that hard to develop and, once you learn the right technique, is actually well within the reach of any man or woman of average or better ability.

Part 3 lists five specific benefits you will gain, simply by putting these techniques, which are contained in this book, to work.

The introduction to this book, therefore, is an attempt to encourage you with these three facts: that the goal you bought this book to attain is worth while, that it is obtain able, and that it will give you the results you wish.

When you have finished this introduction, you know exactly what goals you are out to get. Then, reading on through the table of contents, you realize, step by step, exactly how you are going to get them.

In your one brief survey of this book, or any other, you now know exactly what it is you want to get out of it, and where it is located. You are now ready to read the text itself. To cut through it to the heart of its main ideas, and do it almost as fast as your eyes can move down the page.

Let's now turn to the individual chapters, and see how this same exact method – looking for signposts first – can again mine their information for you at a single glance.

In summary:

No matter how bright you may be, you cannot under stand your assignments simply by reading them word by word.

Instead, you must first *pre-read* those assignments – make a quick survey of them *before* you read to uncover their main thoughts.

You do this, not only with each chapter you are as signed, but with each new book that you study. You find the main ideas of each of these books by checking the following four signpost parts of every book:

1. The title.
2. The table of contents.
3. The index.
4. The introduction or preface.

When you lift these signpost parts out of the text and arrange them in order, you will have at your fingertips an outline of the main thoughts of the entire book.

You can then read each individual chapter in order, with perfect understanding of how it ties into the chapter that has gone before it, the chapter that follows it, and the main theme of the book as a whole.

Now let's see how easy it is to pull out the main thoughts of each chapter in the same exact way.

CHAPTER 8

SIGNPOST PARTS OF EVERY CHAPTER, AND WHAT EACH ONE TELLS YOU

In the section above, when we looked at the four big signposts in every book – the title, the table of contents, the index; and the introduction – we used this book as our example. This technique is used everytime you open a new book.

Using this technique, you get a bird's-eye view of the entire book, the first day you begin it. During the rest of the book, chapter by chapter, you are merely filling in important details, deepening your understanding of the grand plan you discovered in your first survey of the book.

To do this, you apply to each individual chapter the same quick-survey you used at the beginning of the book.

To illustrate this technique in action, let's turn now to three fresh examples – to typical textbooks you will meet in your work.

And let us see exactly what you should do to them, step by step. How much material you have left – and how much you have discarded – when you have finished reducing them to their main thoughts. And how you burn that material into your memory, for good.

Here are these examples, first reproduced word for word (I suggest you simply glance over them briefly now):

CHAPTER FROM A TEXTBOOK ON ENGLISH
THE FOUR KINDS OF SENTENCES

A declarative sentence makes a statement. It is followed by a period.
EXAMPLE: Arthur is an accountant.

An interrogative sentence asks something. It is a question. It is followed by a question mark.
EXAMPLE: Do you have an accountant working for you?

To find the subject of an interrogative sentence, simply turn it into a declarative sentence.
EXAMPLE: You do have an accountant working for you.

An exclamatory sentence shows surprise or excitement. It is followed by an exclamation point.

EXAMPLE: What a thrilling thought!

Sometimes an exclamatory sentence has to be changed to a simple declarative sentence before it is clear what the subject and predicate are.

EXAMPLE:

A. Exclamatory:

How Dick and John hate each other!

B. The same sentence turned into a declarative sentence:

Dick and John hate each other, how.

An imperative sentence gives a command. It is followed by either a period or an exclamation point.

EXAMPLE: Tell me where you were!

In an imperative sentence the word you is always under stood to be the subject.

EXAMPLE: (You) tell me where you were!

FIRST SECTION FROM A CHAPTER IN A TEXTBOOK ON WORLD HISTORY:

(I have numbered each paragraph at the end for reference.)

THE GREEKS

1. The Background

The ancient Greeks developed the first government that might be called democratic and the first great civilization to take permanent root on the mainland of Europe. Yet the Greek civilization that matured almost twenty-five hundred years ago was by no means purely European in character. The Greeks in habited the western coast of Asia Minor and the islands dotting the Aegean Sea as well as the European peninsula we call Greece. They also inherited some of the legacy of the older Near Eastern civilizations, probably passed on to them through the Aegean civilization. (1)

Aegean Civilization

Aegean Civilization, which lasted for some two thousand years down to about 1100 B.C., apparently centered on the island of Crete at the southern entrance to the Aegean Sea. Crete had many natural advantages. Its mild climate favored agriculture; the sea gave it some protection against invasion and conquest and at the same time promoted seafaring. Located at the cross-roads of the Eastern Mediterranean, Crete was close enough to Asia, Africa and Europe for daring seamen to sail their primitive vessels to Egypt and Greece. Its geographical position doubtless made trade and piracy the natural occupations of the islanders. (2)

When copper and the manufacture of bronze were intro duced, probably from Phoenicia or elsewhere in Asia Minor at some time before 3000 B.C., civilization began on Crete. The civilization is termed Minoan, from Minos, a legendary king, and archeologists have divided it into three main chronological periods (3):

Early Minoan – down to 2300 B.C.
Middle Minoan – 2300 to 1600 B.C.
Late Minoan – 1600 to 1100 B.C. (4)

Each of these three main periods is subdivided into three segments, from I to III. The greatest flowering of culture on Crete seems to have occurred during the Middle Minoan III and the late Minoan I and II, between 1700 and 1400 B.C. (5)

We must say "seems to have occurred," for our knowledge of ancient Crete is still incomplete. Up to the beginning of the twentieth century it was so sketchy that no methodical approach to its civilization was possible. Then, in 1900, the British archeologist, Sir Arthur Evans, acting on a well-founded hunch, began excavations at Cnossus in central Crete, a few miles inland from the north shore of the island. He struck "pay-dirt" almost at once and started to uncover what was evidently a very large and very ancient palace, which he termed the "palace of Minos." Subsequent diggings by Evans and others disclosed the sites of more than a hundred towns that had existed before 1500 B.C., a goodly amount of pottery, and stretches of paved road. (6)

More recently, hundreds of tablets with Aegean writing have also come to light, both in Crete itself and on the Greek mainland. Although no Minoan equivalent of the Rosetta stone has been found, one scholar announced in 1953 that by using the techniques of cryptography, he had begun the work of decipher ing the tablets. This discovery may eventually revolutionize our knowledge of Crete. Meanwhile, we have very little sure infor mation on Minoan politics, though it is conjectured that Crete, like Egypt, had despotic priest-kings who ruled with the aid of a central bureaucracy. (7)

The archeological remains, however, provide convincing evidence that the Minoans were great builders, engineers and artists. The Palace at Cnossus was at least two stories high and filled an area equivalent to a city block. A city in miniature, it had runnnig water, a sewage system, and a kind of playground used for dancing, wrestling and other sports. The palace was begun in the Middle Minoan I period and was often repaired and altered, particularly after Middle Minoan II after a destructive earthquake. As a result, the excavated palace is a maze of storerooms, courtyards, corridors, workshops, living quarters and government offices. Sir Arthur Evans realized that he had very likely discovered the actual building that had inspired the Greek legend of the labyrinth to which the early Greeks were forced to send sacrificial victims. (8)

The skilled craftsmen of Crete apparently copied Egyptian techniques. They did marvelous work, from huge jars, as high as a man, to delicate little cups, no thicker than an eggshell, decorated with birds, flowers, fishes and other natural designs. Painters executed large frescos of kings and warriors on the palace walls. Ivory, gold and jewels were used for the inlaid gaming boards of the kings and for exquisite statuettes, less than a foot high, of the bare-breasted snake-goddess, who was apparently one of the chief objects of worship. (9)

Crete at the height of its power may have controlled an empire including the other Aegean islands and, perhaps, the Aegean shores of Asia Minor and Greece. The recent work on Aegean tablets, however, suggests that Crete itself may have become an outpost of the Greek mainland rather early. The extent of Minoan *political* influence is highly uncertain; there is less doubt about Minoan *cultural* influence, which very likely reached to other parts of the Aegean world. (10)

A nineteenth-century German, Heinrich Schliemann, under took excavations at Troy, in northwest Asia Minor, the scene of Homer's *Iliad*, and at Mycenae on the Greek mainland, the home of Agamemnon, the leader of the Greek forces in the Trojan War of Homer's epic. Schliemann's determination resulted in a great archeological romance – early poverty, business success in America, mastery of the Greek language, marriage to a Greek lady (she could recite Homer from memory!), and finally, later in life, discovery of the site of Troy, though it turned out that what he uncovered was a later city built on the ruins of Homeric Troy. (11)

Thanks to Schliemann and later experts, we now know that by 1400 B.C. Troy and a group of cities centered at Mycenae in Greece had attained a degree of civilization strikingly similar to what had apparently been reached in Crete centuries earlier. Mycenaean pottery, though made of different materials, is similar to Minoan in design and ornamentation. At Mycenae, the kings were buried in large underground tombs, shaped like beehives, which resembled tombs built earlier in Crete. The cities on the mainland, however, built much more elaborate fortifications than did those of Crete. (12)

By about 1600 B.C., sporadic groups of invaders were filter ing down from the north. They appear to have been Greeks, a people who spoke a language probably much like the classic Greek. The first Greeks seemed to have mixed rather peaceably with the existing populations of Greece, the Aegean islands, and Asia Minor, and to have acquired the Aegean culture that flourished at Mycenae and elsewhere. Later Greek invaders were more warlike and destructive. As tribe after tribe pushed south, the old Aegean civilization grew steadily weaker until it finally perished about 1100 B.C. By that time, the Greeks controlled the entire Aegean area, including Crete itself. (13)

The Setting of Greek Civilization

The forces of nature played a large part in shaping Greek civilization. The climate and geography of the Greek homeland have changed little since ancient times. As in the Mediterranean area as a whole, the rains come mainly between September and May. The summers are long, sunny and dry,

but because of the sea breezes they are not intolerably hot. People can live outdoors during the greater part of the year, and they can grow olives and other semi-tropical fruit. The sharply indented coastline and the profusion of mountains make a magnificent natural setting. Nature combines such lavish amounts of sunshine and scenery only in California and a few other parts of the world. (14)

Greece, however, has never had the immense fertile acres typical of California. The quality of the soil is poor, and the valleys and plains, squeezed by the mountains, are on a miniature scale. The rivers and streams are too swift and shallow for navigation; they flood in the rainy season, then dwindle to a trickle or dry up altogether. Local springs can supply the minimum needs of the population during the dry season, but they are not adequate for extensive irrigation. (15)

Greece, in short, has never afforded men an easy living, though it has often provided a reasonably pleasant one. The farms and orchards of ancient Greece produced barley and other grains, fruit, wine, honey and little else. Meat was a rarity. (16)

The Greek homeland, however, had one great geographical advantage: its situation encouraged navigation, even by the rather timid. The irregular coasts of the mainland and the islands provided sheltered anchorages; destructive storms seldom occurred during the long summer, the great season of navigation; and the vessels could go for hundreds of miles without ever losing sight of land. Travel in ships propelled by sails or oars or a combination of the two was cheaper, swifter and more comfortable than an up-hill and down-dale journey over land. The Greeks, consequently, built up an active maritime trade. (17)

The geography of Greece favored political decentralization. In the valleys of the Tigris, the Euphrates and the Nile, the absence of natural barriers to travel had helped the building of large empires. In Greece, on the other hand, the frequent mountains and countless bays and gulfs impeded land communication. The individual valleys and plains, both on the mainland and on the islands, were natural geographic and economic units; they served as separate political units, too. (18)

The political unit was the polis or city-state, which included a city and the surrounding countryside. Most of the city-states were exceedingly limited in area; Greece, although a small country, contained many dozens of them. By modern standards, the average Greek city was at best a mere town, and many of its inhabitants were primarily farmers. A strong point, which could be readily defended against attack, was the nucleus of the city. A familiar example is the Acropolis at Athens, with its commanding height and its steep and difficult approaches. (19)

FROM A TEXTBOOK ON BUSINESS ADMINISTRATION

(I have numbered each paragraph at the end for reference.)

CHAPTER 2: FIVE ROADS TO COST REDUCTION

Every management is faced with a continuing need to effect cost reduction. Somehow or other we think of these reductions as available principally in the manufacturing process, but this is not the sole area for expense reduction. There are at least five channels through which important savings can be effected. These are (1):

1. Raw materials.
2. The costs of capital equipment.
3. Manufacturing costs.
4. Sales expense.
5. General and administrative overhead expense (including the office). (2)

Although there are some procedures in common which you can use in endeavoring to reduce expenses along these five ave nues, for the most part the approaches must be different. (3)

Road 1: Raw Materials

Raw materials costs vary greatly with industries. Most com panies have long since worked out the average percentage of the sales dollar paid for raw materials and supplies. If you can make a comparison of this percentage for your company against other companies in your industry, you may have an excellent starting pOint. And even where you can't do this, or the comparison is favorable to your company, it nevertheless may pay you to study the ways of lowering the cost of raw materials. Here are the principal devices which companies have used (4):

1. Development of carefully prepared purchasing specifications, which demand raw material which is good enough for your manufacturing process but not of such high quality that your costs go up without a compensating increase in the price of your ultimate product. (5)

2 . Inspection of incoming materials to make certain that they meet these specifications. (6)

3. Tracing back difficulties in the manufacturing process to raw material imperfections. (7)

4. Modifications of manufacturing processes to eliminate the necessity for certain raw materials and supplies. (8)

5. Substitution of other kinds of raw materials. (9)

6. Control over the sources of raw materials either by pur-· chase of supply sources (vertical integration) or by long term contractual arrangements. (10)

Road 2: The Costs of Capital Equipment

Piled upon manufacturing costs and material costs must be cost of capital equipment used. Typical of such costs would be depreciation, replacement, maintenance and interest on borrowed capital. (ll)

A great many companies tie up a lot of money in semifinished or finished inventories. It's useful to make an occasional check as to the amount so tied up and compare it with previous checks. (12)

Because of inventory pricing policies used by accountants at the close of the year, many a company goes through the year thinking it has had a profitable operation, only to discover that . the inventory pricing has sharply reduced the expected profit. (13)

In Chapter 4 we shall consider capital financing in more detail, so we sball not make further comment here. (14)

Road 3: Manufacturing Costs

Manufacturing costs normally consist of labor plus material plus manufacturing overhead. (15)

Labor opens up a large area for study. It includes proper original selection, adequate training of workers, incentives, supervision, standards and control. It may involve aptitude testing, skill training, time and motion study, work simplification, etc. (16)

Reduction of manufacturing overhead may involve studies of supervision, maintenance and other indirect labor; of inspection and quality control; of fuel, light and power; of fire, safety and insurance protection; of idle equipment charges; of proper utilization of the space available; etc. (17)

Design for new equipment for production involves consideration of manufacturing methods and the capital investment required. (18)

Proper lighting· has been responsible for worthwhile increases in productivity and reduction of accidents. Improvements have also resulted from painting of walls and machines, reduction of noise, better ventilation, etc. (19)

Materials handling is usually another fertile field for investigation. The movement and storage of raw materials, work in progress and finished goods can add conSiderably to the final cost of manufactured goods. (20)

Studies of productive operations may readily include operations research, whereby mathematics is applied to determine the optimum or best manufacturing conditions. Typical would be job lot size to derive the greatest advantage from manufacturing operations; proper inventories of raw materials, partial assemblies, semi-finished products and finished products. (21)

Road 4: Sales Expense

Over the present century there has been a reversal of the relationship of manufacturing costs to marketing costs. At one time manufacturing costs represented more than half the sales price of an article, but these costs have relatively receded so that today, in most companies, the sales costs represent more than half the sales price. Contributing to this increase in sales costs have been such items as warehousing, transportation, advertising, packaging, direct sales costs, and the constant price attrition of competition. Sales overhead, too, has increased through the addition of market research, sales promotion specialists, auto matic vending equipment, more sales supervision. (22)

Many sales managers have virtually become sales controllers. Their functions increasingly are those of analysis and control. They need both the accountant's figures as to sales expense and the statistician's figures as to sales analysis. The latter will normally show dollar and quantity sales by salesman, by territory, by customer and product. Wherever the sales manager detects a falling off in some one of these areas, he applies effort to change the condition. (23)

Road 5: General and Administrative Expense

The fifth avenue of cost reduction consists of analysis of general and administrative expenses. In the normal company these cover such items as salaries of executives and office employees, office expense, interest, property depreciation, taxes, in surance, donations, legal fees, consultants, investigation of pos sible mergers, economic services and other general business expenses. (24)

In Summary:

The five roads to cost reduction are:

1. Raw materials.

2. The costs of capital equipment.

3. Manufacturing costs.

4. Sales Expense.

5. General and administrative expense. (26)

Once possible economies have been uncovered it is necessary to prosecute them vigorously, lest they fail of accomplishment through inertia and resistance to change. (27)

NOW LET'S GET TO WORK ON THOSE CHAPTERS. HERE'S HOW THE CHAPTER SIGNPOSTS BREAK THEM DOWN FOR YOU, IN MINUTES.

As you could tell at a glance, it's simply not enough for you to just read these sample chapters, word by word, from start to finish. If you try to do this, you will confuse detail with main idea, and you will remember almost nothing when you are through reading.

What you need is a key – a system – that will unlock that mass of words and pull out the main ideas for you.

This key is PRE-READING. The ability to read chapter signposts at a glance, and use them to pinpoint the main ideas of the chapter, one after the other, and give purpose and direction to your reading.

There are eight signpost parts of every chapter that you should know as well as your own name. Let's review them one by one, and see how they pull the main ideas right out of these chapters before you begin to read the text.

1. THE CHAPTER TITLE

What it tells you: What the chapter is about. What it includes and does not include.

Examples: In the first chapter, the title The Four Kinds of Sentences show you that there are a specific number of definitions to learn – four. And each of these definitions describes a different kind of sentence. Thus you know immediately what you are looking for – definitions – and how many you must find – four.

The third sample chapter gives the same information in its title. *Five Roads to Cost Reduction* tells you that you must find a specific number of ways to reduce costs – five – and must discover how and in what ways each one works.

The title of the second chapter: *THE GREEKS, I. The Background* is more vague. It does not tell how many parts are to follow. But it does tell you that you are going to study the Greeks, and what you are going to look for in the first section of the chapter is the effect of their background upon them. You must now read on, to the next chapter signposts, to discover what you must find out about their background. To do this, you turn to:

2. THE SECTION HEADINGS

What they tell you: The section headings break down the over-all chapter heading into its main parts. They list the names and number of important subjects to be covered in the chapter. Reading them quickly, without the interven ing text, gives you the skeleton of the chapter.

Examples: The section headings in our third sample chapter read as follows:
> *Road 1: Raw Materials*
> *Road 2: The Costs of Capital Equipment*
> *Road 3: Manufacturing Costs*
> *Road 4: Sales Expense*
> *Road 5: General and Administrative Expense*

Here are the five roads to cost reduction mentioned in the chapter title, laid out for you at a glance. You now know the entire structure of the chapter. Your only task now is to read the text, and find out how you can reduce costs in each of these areas.

In sample Chapter 2, however, the section headings are fewer in number and more vague. They are:
Aegean Civilization, and *The Setting of Greek Civilization*

These give you the two main sources of the background of Greek civilization. But they do not yet give you enough information on what you are to find out about each. There fore you must go on to further signposts, which we will describe in a moment.

And in our first sample chapter, there are no section headings at all. So you check the next chapter signpost, which is:

3. PARAGRAPH HEADS OR BOLD PRINTS

What they tell you: The main topic of each paragraph. What the paragraph contains, boiled down into a single phrase.

For example: In this first sample chapter, the author has carefully stated the name of each kind of sentence.

Listing them in order, we have:
Declarative sentence
Interrogative sentence
Exclamatory sentence
Imperative sentence

Immediately, yon know the names of the four kinds of sentences you are to learn in this lesson. Now all you have to do is read the text, and find out a definition for each of them.

In the other two sample chapters, there are no paragraph headings. And so we turn to the next chapter signpost:

4. INTRODUCTORY PARAGRAPHS

What they tell you: Here the author points out what to look for in the text that follows. He gives an introduction to the chapter, ties it into the chapters that came before it, and reveals the main thought or thoughts in the material in the remainder of the chapter.

For example: In the second sample chapter, the authors begin with this introductory paragraph (for the purposes of this survey, let's break the paragraph apart, point out each of its main thoughts, and state the purpose): *"The ancient Greeks developed the first government that might be called democratic and the first great civilization to take permanent root on the mainland of Europe."* (This is the introduction to the chapter, pointing out the importance of the Greeks to us all.)

"Yet the Greek civilization that matured almost two thousand five hundred years ago was by no means purely European in character."
(Now the authors lead us from the introductory sentence to the non-European background of the Greeks. This is what they are going to discuss in the material that follows.)

"The Greeks inhabited the western coast of Asia Minor and the islands dotting the Aegean Sea as well as the European peninsula we call Greece."
(We are told the first important influence, the geographical setting.)

"They also inherited some of the legacy of the older Near Eastern Civilizations, probably passed on to them through the Aegean Civilization." (And now we are told the second vital influence, the Aegean civilization.)

Thus the introductory paragraph confirms the two main divisions in the chapter-the Aegean Civilization and the Geographical Setting-that were revealed earlier by a survey of the section headings. Now you know you're on the right track. But you're still looking for further subdivisions. So you continue to search to the next chapter signpost.

Usually you would next check:

5. THE SUMMARY OR CLOSING PARAGRAPHS

What they tell you: The summary paragraphs are the author's last words on the chapter. They are his own outline of the material he has covered in this chapter before he passes on to the next. They are a declaration of what *he* deems important out of all the material you have just read.

Sometimes he sums this material up in one paragraph. Sometimes he outlines each idea in a separate phrase, paragraphs it, and may even number it. Sometimes he rephrases the important points in the form of questions.

In any case, these final words deserve careful study before you begin the text.

For example: Since there is no summary paragraph in our second sample chapter, let's use the one in the third chapter as our example. It reads:

> *"In Summary:*
>
> *The five roads to cost reduction are:*
> *1. Raw Materials.*
> *2 . The Costs of Capital Equipment.*
> *3. Manufacturing Costs.*
> *4. Sales Expense.*
> *5. General and Administrative Expense.*
>
> *Once possible economies have been uncovered, it is necessary to prosecute them vigorously, lest they fail of accomplishment through inertia and resistance to change."*

These sentences confirm what you have already discovered. You are now doubly sure that you have the five roads to cost reduction firmly outlined in your mind; and, especially on the basis of the last paragraph in the summary, now only have to read on to discover how you can reduce costs in each of these areas.

You now turn to the next chapter signpost:

6. THE FIRST SENTENCE OF EACH PARAGRAPH

What they tell you: As you remember, this Pre-Reading, this quick survey of an entire chapter before you begin the text, is essentially a search. A search for the main thoughts of that chapter-for a quick outline of that chapter that tells you exactly what you are looking for and where to find it.

This search begins with the chapter title, and continues, one by one, with each of the following chapter signposts till you have uncovered those main ideas – till you have built your outline.

At this point, when you have located the main ideas in the chapter, you stop the Pre-Reading and begin the text. The Pre-Reading is a search for the chapter's main ideas. When you have found them, you begin to read.

Therefore you do not check all the chapter signposts in each Pre-Reading of each chapter. You check only enough signposts to give you your main ideas, and then ignore the others.

For example, in the first sample chapter, you needed only to read the chapter title, then check to see that there were no section headings, and then simply pick up your main ideas out of the underlined paragraph headings. At that point, you had the four kinds of sentences, and would immediately begin to read the text to find a definition for each.

However, it is the second sample chapter that forces you to make a deeper survey. In this second chapter, you have read the title, found only two section headings, found no paragraph heads, discovered that the introductory paragraph merely confirms the two main ideas you learned from the section headings, and again found that there was no summary paragraph.

So what you have gained from your first five signposts is this. You know that you are to learn about the background of Greek civilization. And you know that there are two sources of this background – the Aegean civilization, and the geographical setting of Greece.

What you still do not know, however, *is what each of these sources contributed* to Greek civilization. You have to uncover these contributions – how many there were and what each of them was – before you can begin reading with definite clear-cut goals in mind.

Therefore, you probe deeper. You turn to the next chapter signpost – the first sentence of each paragraph.

In most cases, especially if the author has done his work well, these first sentences are called *topic sentences.* They give the main idea of the paragraph, and let the remaining sentences fill in the details.

So, if you take the first sentence of each paragraph and string them together, you should have a fairly good outline of the main ideas in the chapter.

Unfortunately, this method is not as automatic or as clear cut as those using the first five signposts. You have to use more judgment in weeding out paragraphs that don't really contain main ideas.

But in those rare cases when the first five signposts don't do the job, you must go on with the sixth. Let's see how this method opens up the main ideas in this massive second chapter:

For example: The first sentences of each paragraph in the second chapter are these. (We will give each sentence the number of the paragraph it comes from. And we will leave out the first, introductory sentence, since we have already covered it):

"*AEGEAN CIVILIZATION*

2. *Aegean civilization, which lasted for some two thousand yem's down to about 1100 B.C., apparently centered on the island of Crete at the southern entrance to the Aegean Sea.*

3. *When the copper and the manufacture of bronze were introduced, probably from Phoenicia or elsewhere in Asia Minor at some time before 3000 B.C., civilization began on Crete.*

4. (Unimportant)

5. (Unimportant)

6. (Unimportant)

7. (Unimportant)

8. *The archeological remains, however, provide convincing evidence that the Minoans were great builders, engineers and artists.*

9. (Unimportant)

10. *Crete at the height of its power may have controlled an empire including the other Aegean islands and, perhaps, the Aegean shores of Asia Minor and Greece.*

11. (Unimportant)

12. *Thanks to Schliemann and later experts, we now know that by 1400 B.C. Troy and a group of cities centered at Mycenae in Greece had attained a degree of civilization strikingly similar to what had apparently been reached in Crete centuries earlier.*

13. (Unimportant)

THE SETTING OF GREEK CIVILIZATION
14. *The forces of nature played a large part in shaping Greek civilization.*
15. (Unimportant)
16. (Unimportant)
17. *The Greek homeland, however, had one great geographical advantage: its situation encouraged navigation, even by the very timid.*
18. *The geography of Greece favored political decentralization.*
19. (Unimportant)"

These are the first sentences of each important paragraph in the chapter. Already, in choosing them, the boiling-down process has begun. Already unnecessary words and details have been thrown away. You are looking only for main ideas. You therefore choose only those paragraphs that contain those main ideas.

Rut how do you know which paragraph to choose and which to leave out? In a very simple way.

You already know the main theme of the chapter, THE GREEKS, *1. The background,* which was given to you in the chapter title.

You already know the two main sources of that back ground, *Aegean Civilization and the Geographical Setting,* which were given to you in the section headings.

You do not know, however, how many divisions each of these two sources have, and what each contributed to Greek civilization. This is the information you are looking for in the first sentence of each paragraph.

And you are looking only for big contributions, not details.

Therefore you will judge each sentence by these two simple rules:

1. They must talk about the main theme of the chapter, and not about some side issue.
In this case, they must talk about the Aegean contribution to the background of Greek civilization, or about the geographical contribution to that background, and about nothing else.

2. They must bring in a new main point, and not merely furnish details about a main point brought up by the paragraph before.
These are the two rules of what to leave in and what to throw out. They are quite simple to follow. Let's see how they eliminate most of the paragraphs in this second sample chapter, and leave only the main points.

Sentence 2: Mentions Crete as the center of Aegean civilization. Leave it in.

Sentence 3: Shows high civilization, based on metals, that Crete contributed to Greeks. Leave it in.

Sentence 4: Just dates of Minoan culture. No contribution to Greeks. Throw it out.

Sentence 5: More Minoan periods. Out.

Sentence 6: Says nothing but that our knowledge of Crete is incomplete. No contribution here. Probably a side issue. Throw it out.

Sentence 7: Another scientific side issue. Out.

Sentence 8: Now we get to basic contributions from the Minoans – building, engineering, artistry. Leave it in.

Sentence 9: Details about Minoan art. We already have art in the sentence above. Leave it out.

Sentence 10: Discusses Minoan seafaring, politics, war – all picked up by Greeks later on. Leave it in.

Sentence 11: Side issue. Interesting but not important. Throw it out.

Sentence 12: Identifies other centers of Aegean civilization. Now we know there were two – Crete and Mycenae. And we know that they both made essentially the same contributions. A good find. Leave it in.

Sentence 13: Talks about invaders, not Aegeans. Not on topic we want. Throw it out.

Sentence 14: Identifies forces of nature as first great geographical influence of Greeks. Leave it in.

Sentence 15: Detail under natural forces (soil condi tions). Leave it out.

Sentence 16: Mere comment on effect of natural forces. Covered already by sentence 14 above. Out.

Sentence 17: New effect of geographical setting – navigable water. Important. Leave it in.

Sentence 18: A third main effect – political decentralization. Leave it in.

Sentence 19: A detail about the political centralization mentioned in the paragraph above – the name of the citystate. Not a main point. Throw it out.

Now what have you left, after you've thrown out the unimportant paragraphs? Let's see.

Taking the title and section headings as they are, and further boiling down the first sentences to a phrase or two each, this is what you should end up with:

THE GREEKS, I. BACKGROUND

Aegean Civilization.
> *Located at Crete, Troy and Mycenae. All made the same contributions. Contributions were in metals, building, engineering, art, politics, seafaring, warfare.*

The Setting of Greek Civilization.
> *Greek civilization was shaped by (1) the forces of nature; (2) by the easily navigable waters surrounding Greece; and (3) by the Greek terrain, which made for political decentralization.*

With this outline at your fingertips, you now begin reading the text to make sure you understand each of these main points thoroughly.

However, had you not been able to get all the main points from the first six chapter signposts, you still had two more that might have been able to help you. Let's briefly glance at these now:

7. ILLUSTRATIONS

What they tell you: Illustrations, charts, graphs, photographs, etc., are pictorial presentations of the main ideas in each chapter. They boil down great amounts of information, and give them to you at a single glance. Often they convey information that simply could never be put into words.

For example: The map in sample chapter two shows at geographical setting of Greece quite vividly. At a glance, you see the wonderful advantages Greek mariners had to explore the entire Mediterranean. This confirms the main idea shown in the outline above concerning the easily navigable waters surrounding Greece.

And our last chapter signpost:

8. MARGINAL TITLES

What they tell you: Marginal titles take the main point of each paragraph, and set it in bold type in the margin next to the text of the paragraph. They thus build a walking outline of the chapter for you in the margin. Unfortunately, however, they are not used in modern textbooks to any great extent; and you must get the same information from the paragraph headings mentioned above.

For example: None of our three sample chapters uses marginal titles. However, if our second sample chapter did use them, it would look like this:

BEGINNINGS OF MINOAN CIVILIZATION	3. *'When copper and the manufacture of bronze were introduced, probably from Phoenicia or elsewhere in Asia Minor at some time before 3000 B.C., civilization began on Crete. The civilization is termed Minoan, from Minos, a legendary king, and archeologists have divided it into three main chronological periods . . .*

In summary:

When you are reading an individual chapter or lesson in a book, you use the same Pre-Reading, quick-survey technique that you first used to understand the book as a whole.

You use this quick-survey technique to pull out the main ideas from the chapter before you begin to read it.

You find these main ideas by checking the following eight chapter signposts:
1. The Chapter Title.
2. The Section Headings.
3. The Paragraph Headings or Rold Prints.
4. The Introductory Paragraphs.
5. The Summary Paragraphs.
6. The First Sentence of Each Paragraph.
7. The Illustrations.
8. The Marginal Titles.

When you lift these chapter signposts out of the text and arrange them in order, you will have an outline of the main thoughts of that chapter at your fingertips. You may then flash-read that chapter – merely skim ming over the unimportant details – and concentrating only on definite information on each of these main thoughts.

We now turn to a simple trick that will automatically show you exactly what information you must look for on each one of these main points.

CHAPTER 9

HOW TO TURN THE CHAPTER'S MAIN THOUGHTS INTO QUESTIONS, TO AUTOMATICALLY PINPOINT THE INFORMATION YOU NEED ABOUT THEM

Now let's list the outlines you have built by Pre-Read ing the three sample chapters in this book. In the first sample chapter your outline will be as simple as this:

THE FOUR KINDS OF SENTENCES

1. Declarative sentence.
2. Interrogative sentence.
3. Exclamatory sentence.
4. Imperative sentence.

In the second sample chapter, this is the outline you've worked out:

THE GREEKS, I. BACKGROUND

Aegean Civilization.

Located at Crete, Troy and Mycenae. All made the same contributions. Contributions were in metals, building, engineering, politics, seafaring, warfare.

The Setting of Greek Civilization.

Greek civilization was shaped by:
1. The forces of nature.
2. The easily navigable waters surrounding Greece.
3. The Greek terrain, which made for political decentralization.

And in the third sample chapter, the outline emerged like this:

FIVE ROADS TO COST REDUCTION

1. Raw Materials.
2. Capital Equipment.
3. Manufacturing Costs.
4. Sales Expense.
5. General and Administrative Expense.

At this point, you have the main ideas of each sample chapter at your fingertips. Rut your knowledge of the chapter is, of course, still incomplete. Now you must read the text itself, *to find out what you should know about each one of these main points.*

And how do you tell – again in advance of actually reading the text – exactly what it is that you should know about each one of these points?

The answer is simplicity itself. You merely

1. Turn each one of these main points into a question.

And then

2. Read the text to find out their answers.

It's as easy as that. Now let's see this question-and-answer technique in action.

THE SIX BASIC QUESTIONS

Any idea – any word, any phrase, any sentence – can be turned into a question simply by putting in front of it one of these six little words:

> What?
> Why?
> Where?
> When?
> Who?
> How?

These are extremely valuable words. You should memorize them from this moment on. They have been called, and rightly so, the Six Tiny Keys to Knowledge. Let's see what they can do when we apply them to the main thoughts in each one of our sample chapters.

TURNING THE FIRST SAMPLE OUTLINE INTO A SERIES OF QUESTIONS

First, you start with the chapter title. Placing the word what in front of it, you get:

What are the four kinds of sentences?

This question has already been answered for you by the section headings in your outline – declarative, interrogative, exclamatory, and imperative. So you put the same question to each of these four kinds of sentences, like this:

What is the definition of a declarative sentence?
What is the definition of an interrogative sentence?
What is the definition of an exclamatory sentence?
What is the definition of an imperative sentence?

You now know exactly what information you are look ing for about each one of your main points. You now read to answer these questions, to discover that information, and skim over everything else.

TURNING THE SECOND SAMPLE OUTLINE INTO A SERIES OF QUESTIONS

Again, you first start with the chapter title. Placing the word what in front of it, you get:

What are the background sources of Greek civilization?

This question has already been answered for you in the two section headings – the Aegean civilization and the geographical setting. So you question each one of the section headings in turn, like this:

Placing the word where in front of the first section heading, you get:

Where was Aegean civilization located?

Your paragraph headings answer this question – at Crete, Troy and Mycenae. So you ask again:

What were their contributions to Greek civilization?

Again you have the answers – in metals, building, engineering, politics, seafaring, warfare. So you ask again:

What did the Aegean civilization contribute to the Greek Civilization in metals?
What did it contribute in building?
What did it contribute in engineering?
What did it contribute in politics?
What did it contribute in seafaring?
What did it contribute in warfare?

These are the questions in this section that you will read on to answer. You then turn to the second section, and question its heading.

What were the geographical factors that helped shape Greek civilization?

You have your answers – forces of nature, navigable waters, rough terrain. So you question each one of these factors in turn.

How did the forces of nature help shape Greek civilization?
How did navigable waters help shape Greek civilization?
How did the rough terrain help shape Greek civilization?

You now know exactly what information you are looking for about each one of your main points. You now read to answer these questions, to discover that information, and skim over everything else.

TURNING THE THIRD SAMPLE CHAPTER INTO A SERIES OF QUESTIONS

Once again, you first start with the chapter title. Placing the word what in front of if, you get:

What are the five roads to cost reduction?

Your section headings give you the answers-raw materials, capital equipment, manufacturing costs, sales expense, and general and administrative expenses. So you question each one of these section headings in tum, like this:

How can my firm cut raw materials costs?
How can my firm cut capital equipment costs?
How can my firm cut manufactu.ring costs?
How can my firm cut sales costs?
How can my firm cut general and administrative costs?

You now know exactly what information you are looking for about each one of your main points. You now read to answer these questions, to discover this information, and skim over everything else.

In summary:

In order to Pre-Read a chapter or an assignment, you follow three steps:

1. You check the chapter signposts.

2. You use them to pull out the main thoughts of the chapter.

3. You turn those main ideas into questions.

You do this by placing the words, *what, why, where, when, how,* or *who* in front of the thoughts.

And when you have turned them into questions in this way, you then read the text to answer those questions, and skim over everything else.

Let us now see how you slash through that text, mastering its content, without repetition, in a single flash reading.

CHAPTER 10

HOW TO POWER-READ –
MASTER AN ASSIGNMENT IN MINUTES

You have now finished your quick survey of the chapter. You have pulled out its main thoughts and turned them into questions. You are now ready to read the text, word by word, to answer these questions.

Let's see how you do this, in the shortest possible time, without missing a single vital point.

HOW TO DOUBLE YOUR READING RATE

Always, of course, our first goal is to improve your ability to understand everything you read. Rut this search for understanding does not conflict with a second vital goal – to speed up your reading rate.

Fast readers are good readers. And most people who read slowly do so because of one or two crippling habits they've picked up in their school years. Eliminate those habits and you liberate tremendous new-reading speed in yourself overnight.

Since you will be faced with a flood of paperwork in your lifetime, now is the time to build in that speed. Here are five simple tricks that will do it for you automatically:

1. Don't let yourself point out words with your finger or a pencil. This slows you up. *Read with your eyes only.* This means your hands must be folded till you turn to the next page.

2. Keep from moving your lips or mouth. Lip-moving slows reading speed down to speaking speed. If it's difficult for you to stop moving your lips, bite a pencil while you read till you lose the habit.

3. Don't move your head from side to side. This tires you out and again slows up your reading. *Only your eyes should move. Only your eyes need move.*

4. Read aggressively. Actively. Tearing the ideas out of the pages with the techniques we are showing you in this book.

5. Learn the habit of skimming and then concentrating as described below.

Make every reading assignment a search for main thoughts through a forest of useless words. Skim through 90 per cent of those words, and concentrate only on the vital 10 per cent.

And then practice. Practice – practice – practice. Till you become an expert. Till these habits become second nature. Till you can zip through any written page, anywhere.

Like this:

HOW TO FLASH-READ.
CUT THROUGH UNIMPORTANT DETAILS IN SECONDS

Now with these speed-reading skills firmly implanted in your mind as automatic habits, you begin to attack the chapter, word by word.

You begin to read as fast as you can. You read every word. *But now you are sifting those words – judging them – accepting them or rejecting them.*

You are looking for specific answers to specific questions – the questions you constructed in your quick survey before you began to read.

These questions are burned into your mind:

> *What is the definition of a declarative sentence?*
> *How did the forces of nature help shape Greek civilization?*
> *How can my firm cut raw materials costs?*

Every word, every phrase, every sentence that your eye flashes over is judged by whether they answer or do not answer those questions.

If they answer the question, you stop, concentrate, underline as shown below.

If they do not answer the questions, you read on, searching for your answers.

In this way, you merely skim over 90 per cent of the text – the unimportant 90 per cent – the excess details, the side issues, the interesting opinions and prejudices that will never be needed again.

You read them quickly, once. You skip none of them. You let them register in your brain as they will. You let them fill in the details of the vital points you will later concentrate on. You make no deliberate conscious effort to memorize any of them.

But – because at the same time you are building up a structure of one vital thought in the chapter after another – you will find that these skimmed-over details, somehow automatically, stick to these main thoughts.

You will find that you remember far more of this chapter – main thoughts and details both – than you have ever remembered before.

The reason for this increase in memory is simple. We remember what we can understand and what we can organize. If we try to memorize nonsense words or jumbled sentences, for example, we find it almost impossible. And a chapter that is not broken down into main thoughts and details is really nothing but a meaningless jumble.

But once you pick out its main thoughts and put them in order, you have constructed a *memory framework.* From that moment on you have a logical structure, a definite pigeonhole, for details to attach themselves to in your memory.

Then, even though you skim over these details and concentrate only on consciously memorizing your main thoughts, *the details logically stick along to their parent thoughts, and you get them in your mind as a sort of no-work bonus.*

So you have now flash-read 90 per cent of the chapter – simply glanced at the details to pick them up – and are now ready to go to work on your main thoughts. Here's how you do it.

THE MAGIC KEY TO CONCENTRATION

As you remember, you are reading to find specific answers to specific questions. Every sentence you read is judged on that basis. Does it answer your questions, or does it not?

If it does not, you flash-read it, and search on for your answers.

If it does, however, you slow down, concentrate full attention on that sentence, *and pick up your pencil to under line the answer.*

This deliberate physical act – this aggressive under lining of answers in the textbook as they are read – is the Golden Rule that makes your concentration automatic.

It converts routine reading into active, physical thought.

It prevents your mind from wandering. It makes the dead, lifeless material in the book come to life with the thrill of personal discovery. It forces you to evaluate, weed out, judge, emphasize. It is the first great step in turning that material into your own personal acquisition as you hammer it out, answer by answer by answer.

And it is as easy as ABC. There is only one simple procedure to follow.

Every time you find the answer to one of your questions, you simply:
a. Read it carefully.
b. Make sure you understand it.
c. Underline once the specific words you're going to use to remember it.

That's all there is to it. On an entire page you may underline only one or two sentences. In a complete lesson, you may make only four or five marks in your book.

But these physical marks are your own personal mile stones along the road to mastery of that lesson. They are the first active step, not only to locating the vital thoughts of that chapter, *but to making those thoughts part of your mental inventory for as long as you wish to use them.*

Let's see how this underlining process takes place. Let's put it to work on each of our three sample chapters.

HOW TO POWER-READ THE FIRST SAMPLE CHAPTER

Let's take the first paragraph of the first sample chapter. Here's how it now stands in the textbook:

"A declarative sentence makes a statement. It is followed by a period."

Here's how it should look when you have finished read ing it:

"A *declarative* sentence *makes a statement.* It is followed by a period."

You have underlined four words and weeded out the rest. You now know the first kind of sentence and its definition. You have answered your first question. You now go on to the second, and the third, and the fourth, till you have finished the lesson.

HOW TO POWER-READ THE SECOND SAMPLE CHAPTER

In this chapter, let's take paragraph 17 as our example. Here's how it now stands in the textbook:

"The Greek homeland, however, had one great geographical advantage: its situation encouraged navigation, even by the rather timid. The irregular coasts of the mainland and the islands provided sheltered anchorages; destructive storms seldom occurred during the long summer, the great season of navigation; and the vessels could go for hundreds of miles without ever losing sight of land. Travel in ships propelled by sails or oars or a combination of the two was cheaper, swifter and more comfortable than an up hill and down-dale journey overland. The Greeks, consequently, built up an active maritime trade."

As you remember, your Pre-Reading survey had already established the question you were searching for in this section. Here is that question:

How did navigable waters help shape Greek civilization?

With that question in mind, here is how this same paragraph should look when you have finished reading it:

"The Greek homeland, however, had one great geographical advantage: its situation encouraged *navigation*, even by the rather timid. The irregular coasts of the mainland and the islands provided sheltered anchorages; destructive storms seldom occurred during the long summer, the great season of navigation; and the vessels could go for hundreds of miles without ever losing sight of land. Travel in ships propelled by sail or oars or a combination of the two was cheaper, swifter and more comfortable than an up-hill and down-dale journey overland. The Greeks, consequently, *built up an active maritime trade."*

You have underlined eight words, and weeded out the rest. These eight words answer your question completely – allow you to realize that *the navigable waters surrounding Greece enabled the Greeks to build up an active maritime trade.* This is the main thought of this paragraph. The rest is merely detail.

And so you continue with your reading, using this same technique to weed out 95 per cent of the unimportant words in the chapter; to concentrate only on the answers to your main-thought questions; and to build up, answer by answer, the complete, easily remembered Main Thought Outline of this lesson, which we will examine in the next chapter.

HOW TO POWER-READ THE THIRD SAMPLE CHAPTER

As a contrast, let's take paragraph 24 of this chapter.

Here's how it stands in the textbook:

"The fifth avenue of cost reduction consists of analysis of general and administrative expenses. In the normal company these cover such items as salaries of executives and office employees, office expenses, interest, property depreciation, taxes, insurance, donations, legal fees, consultants, investigations of possible mergers, economic services and other general business expenses."

As you remember, the question we were using here was:

How can my firm cut general and administrative costs?

With that question in mind, here is how this same paragraph looks when you have finished it:

"The fifth avenue of cost reduction consists of analysis of *general and administrative expenses.* In the normal company these cover such items as *salaries* of executives and office employees, *office expenses, interest, property depreciation, taxes, insurance, donations, legal fees, consultants, investigations* of possible mergers, economic *services* and *other* general business expenses."

Here the answer to the question gives eleven or more ways to cut costs in this area, and all are underlined. Later, when you build your Main Thought Outline, you will combine several of them so they can be more easily memorized.

At the present point, however, you continue to read on until you have finished the chapter, answered each of your questions and thoroughly understand each of its main points.

In summary:

Once you have made your Pre-Reading survey, with its questions to be answered, the actual reading of the lesson becomes incredibly fast and easy.

During this reading, you will skim over about go percent of the text, searching only for the answers to your mainthought questions, and letting their details stick to your memory automatically.

And when you find a main-thought answer, you actively underline it, marking each word that you will use later to remember it by.

In this way, you actively build up a series of mainthought answers, *which you will now use to build a Main Thought Outline in your notebook so you can remember them as long as you wish.*

It is to this last step of rewriting and remembering that we now turn.

CHAPTER 11

NOTE TAKING – HOW TO REMEMBER WHAT YOU'VE READ AND PUT IT TO IMMEDIATE USE

You are now ready for the pay-off, the moment when you master the meaning of the chapter and make it your own.

What have you done so far? All this:

1. Picked out the main thoughts of the chapter.
2. Turned them into questions.
3. Weeded out material that did not answer those questions, and which you will never have to look at again.
4. Located the answers to those questions – the vital information that composes the backbone of that book.
5. Marked that vital information separate from the rest of the chapter.

You now have everything you need to know about every main thought in that chapter right at your fingertips. Now you have to fit them together.

Now you rewrite the chapter, in your own personal language, making fifty words do the work of five thousand.

YOUR NOTEBOOK, WHERE YOU RE-CREATE THE BACKBONE MEANING OF EACH CHAPTER, EACH BOOK, EACH COURSE

In addition to your own mind, you have only three basic tools to open up the entire world of knowledge to your grasp:

> Your textbook.
> Your pencil.
> And your notebook.

In fact, future advancement may very well depend on your ability to transfer knowledge from one of these books to the other.

What exactly is this notebook of yours? What should it contain? How should it be arranged? How exactly do you use it to get the maximum benefit from your reading?

Let's look at each of the points in turn.

Your notebook is the actual storehouse of all that you have learned, from every one of your books. That notebook should be large and loose-leafed. It should have a durable hard cover. It should have plastic colored separators for each section or book. It should have your name, address, and telephone number written in ink inside the front cover, because it is much too valuable to lose.

When you sit down at your table at home at night, it should be the first book you open. It is your portable organizer. It sets up your entire study schedule, in this way:

If you are going to an adult education class, for example, or taking a correspondence course, each course in the notebook must be set off by a plastic colored separator. The first page following that separator is the assignment page for that course. On that page, each assignment for each day is copied down exactly as it is given by your teacher, like this:

Chapter 2: "Five Roads to Cost Reduction." Pages 64 to 69. Answer questions 1 to 8 at end of chapter, to hand in tomorrow.

Each day's assignments are written in this way on the assignment page, one after another. As they are completed, they are checked off with a red pencil. But they are kept in the notebook, to serve as part of the flash review you will make before you take any test.

HOW YOU WRITE UP EACH DAY'S LESSON IN YOUR NOTEBOOK

After the assignment page, for each course, come the Main Thought Outline pages you will write up, day after day, as you master that course.

These pages are not haphazard in any way. They are not written in the classroom, not written while you are actually reading the text. There is no room on them for illegible scrawls, written daydreaming, or doodles of any kind. They are carefully and precisely prepared, in this way:

1. When you have finished reading the chapter, and when you have underlined the answers to the main-thought questions that you have previously prepared, you then close the book.

2. You are now ready to put your knowledge of the backbone of that chapter to its first test. To do this, you take a blank sheet of paper – not in your notebook – and from memory you write down each of the main thoughts of that chapter and the information you have learned about them.

3. You will forget some these points. You will write down some of them out of order. You will find that you still don't clearly understand some of the information about them. None of this is important. What is important is the fact that you have just made your first recitation, taken your first self-test on that chapter.

4. You now go back to the text and check and correct your outline. You write the corrections directly onto that rough outline.

5. When you have finished it, when you have boiled down and correctly arranged to your own satisfaction, then you turn that paper over. You open your notebook. And you write that outline – again from memory – on one page of that notebook.

6. What you are doing is freeing yourself, step by step, from the crutch of that textbook. You are transferring knowledge out of that textbook into your own memory, and then into your notebook for instant reference. And each step of the way you are condensing that knowledge, memorizing and rememorizing it, understanding it more deeply and clearly with each word you write.

7. When you have finished writing the outline in your notebook, you check it again. If there are one or two errors or omissions, write them in. If there are too many, rewrite the entire page. Write on only one side of the paper, how ever, because you will use the other side later to double the profit you get out of every hour of review.

And then, when you have the outline in your notebook finished to your satisfaction, close both books and finish for the night. You have learned your chapter. You have the backbone of that chapter stored in your memory and your notebook, ready to go to work for you at an instant's notice.

Let's see what these finished outlines should look like, for each one of our sample chapters:

THE FINISHED OUTLINE FOR OUR FIRST SAMPLE CHAPTER

THE FOUR KINDS OF SENTENCES:

1. Declarative – makes a statement.

2. Interrogative – asks something.

3. Exclamatory – shows surprise or excitement.

4. Imperative – gives a command.

THE FINISHED OUTLINE FOR OUR SECOND SAMPLE CHAPTER

THE GREEKS, I. THE BACKGROUND

1. Aegean Civilization.

> *Centered at Crete, Troy, Mycenae.*
>
> *Contributions were:*
>
>> *a. Copper and bronze basis for high civilization.*
>>
>> *b. Advanced engineering techniques produced fortifications and palaces.*
>>
>> *c. Ruled by kings.*
>>
>> *d. Empire building through trade and warfare by sea.*

2. Geographical Influences:

> *Poor soil and climate forced Greeks to seek their fortunes overseas.*
>
> *Easy navigability made sea transportation easier and more profitable than land.*
>
> *Rough terrain encouraged individual city-states.*

THE FINISHED OUTLINE FOR OUR THIRD SAMPLE CHAPTER

FIVE ROADS TO COST REDUCTION

1. Cut raw materials cost by:

> *a. Precise purchasing specifications.*
>
> *b. Inspection of incoming materials.*
>
> *c. Elimination of manufacturing difficulties due to raw materials.*
>
> *d. Substitution or elimination of unnecessary materials.*
>
> *e. Financial control of sources.*

2. Cut capital equipment costs by:

> *a. Reducing costs of depreciation, replacement, maintenance and interest.*
>
> *b. Holding down inventories.*
>
> *c. Sharpening accounting procedures.*

3. Cut manufacturing costs by:

> *a. Better labor management.*
>
> *b. Analysis of* indirect costs.
>
> *c. Design of new equipment.*
>
> *d. Better working conditions.*

  e. Improved materials handling.

  f. Operations research.

4. Cut sales costs by cutting costs of:

  a. Warehousing.

  b. Transportation.

  c. Advertising.

  d. Packaging.

  e. Direct sales costs.

  f. New specialist costs.

5. Cut general and administrative costs:

  a. Administrative salaries.

  b. Office expense.

  c. Interest.

  d. Insurance.

  e. Donations

  f. Legal fees.

  g. Consultants and other economic services.

TIPS ON IMPROVING YOUR OUTLINES

1. Simplify. Keep compressing, boiling down, making the outline shorter and shorter. Use phrases instead of sentences. Eliminate unnecessary words and details. Blend subordinate sentences into others by boiling them down into one or two words. Keep cutting till each idea stands sharp and clear in a few easy-to-remember words.

2. Fit the ideas together properly. Make sure one leads into the other in the right order. Then, when you think of the first idea, the second automatically pops into your mind.

3. What are the kinds of order you can use to make one idea fit in with another? Here are a few:

A. Parts of Something.

Example:

  Kinds of birds:

  1. Sparrow.

  2. Robin.

  3. Bluebird, etc.

B. Time Order.

Example:

Battles of World War II:

1. Poland.

2. Holland.

3. France.

4. Britain, etc.

C. Step-by-Step Sequence.
Example:

How to Build a Work Bench:

1. Check each part and arrange in order.

2. Read instructions carefully.

3. Cut out all parts, etc.

D. Causes of Something.
Example:

Causes of 1929 Depression:

1. Watered stock.

2. Insufficient government control.

3. Speculation by banks, etc.

E. Effects of Something.
Example:

Results of 1929 Depression:

1. Vast unemployment.

2. Business bankruptcies.

3. Loss of 1932 election, etc.

F. Arrangement by Space.
Example:

States on the Eastern Seaboard:

1. Maine.

2. Vermont.

3. New Hampshire.

4. Rhode Island, etc.

These are only a few samples. Look for other kinds, and keep a list of them at the back of your notebook.

4. Use numbers. They are a great help, both in under standing a lesson and remembering it for future use. For example, once you know that there are five roads to cost reduction, you realize that you must reproduce all five of them on

any future test. If you had not numbered them, however, you may have thought there were only four, and left one out because you didn't stop to search for it.

5. Indent. And then indent again. Physical indentions show instantly the difference between the theme of the entire chapter and its sub-thoughts. And if these sub-ideas have any further divisions, again indentions show their relation at a glance. Notes should be neat and precise, with plenty of white space around each point, so you can see exactly where it stands in relation to the chapter as a whole when you review it.

HOW TO USE YOUR NOTES

When you finish writing up these notes each night, you have accomplished not one but two vital tasks:

1. You have read and understood the chapter assigned to you – and understood it more completely than you have ever dreamed before.

2. You have stored away the backbone meaning of that chapter – *so that you can now thoroughly review it for a test by reading as few as fifty words, instead of as many as five thousand.*

You have two enormous advantages over every other person in your class who does not use this technique. And you begin putting those advantages to use immediately.

Your first review takes place right after you finish those notes, in your ten-minute review that same evening. Here you discover exactly how much you have gained from your day's reading. Here you put this new knowledge to work before you even enter your class the next evening.

The procedure is simple. You put away your notes, then try to rewrite them from memory.

You should be able to write all those notes from memory, without referring back to your original copy. If not, reread the original notes until each point in them is clear in your mind.

Then test your over-all mastery of the course by asking yourself these questions, which force you to tie in your daily reading with everything you have learned before:

"Why did the author place this chapter where it is in the book?"

"How does it tie in with the chapter I read yesterday?"

"What did I have to know in yesterday's chapter before I could understand the material I read today?"

These questions force you to think. To tie in. To relate forward and backward. And to become accustomed to expressing your thoughts in your own words.

When you are through with that simple review each night, you know that you have mastered that material. And you're confident that you talk sense about it to anyone.

THE NEXT EVENING

And the next evening, on your way to class, take one more brief look over these notes. Driving to school, walking through the halls, with your notebook closed, run through these three magic questions:

"In one sentence, what did I learn from last night's chapter?" (That the five roads to cost reduction are through reducing raw materials costs, manufacturing costs, capital equipment costs, sales costs, and general and administrative costs.)

"How does this tie in with the chapter before?" (It's a second way of increasing profits, right after improved management.)

"What questions will I be asked on it in next week's test?" (To list several ways of reducing costs in each one of these areas. And run through them.)

Using this planning technique, in half the time that it would have taken you to read that chapter before, you are now ready to go in that classroom and make your friends' eyes pop open in amazement.

In summary:

There is an easy, simple, organized way to master the contents of any assignment. It consists of the following three steps:

1. Pre-Read the assignment, to pick out its main thoughts and tum them into questions.

2. Power-read the assignment, to weed out unnecessary details and concentrate on the answers to these questions.

3. Translate the assignment into a Main Thought Outline that expresses these answers in as few words as possible, and that is stored for instant review in your notebook.

These are the three Magic Keys to Expert Reading.

You should practice them again and again and again, until they become second nature. They will pay you dividends for the rest of your life.

CHAPTER 12

HOW TO GET TWICE AS MUCH OUT
OF YOUR DAILY READING

Now let's put these reading skills to work for you in another area.

Let's see how they can save you time and effort every single day. Double the amount of information you get out of a magazine or newspaper. Cut your business reading time in half. Let you flash right through the latest best-seller and dazzle your friends that same evening with the insights you have into everyone of its events and characters.

Let's start with the Number One source of information for most people - your newspaper:

HOW THE PROFESSIONALS READ THEIR NEWSPAPER

You need two separate skills-two separate patterns of action-to get the most out of your daily paper:

1. How to read your newspaper as a whole.

2. How to read each individual news story that catches your eye.

First, let's set up an over-all pattern of attack-a timed, step-by-step procedure-that will tear out all the important facts from your paper for you every evening or morning.

Here's how we do it- step by step:

1. When you open your newspaper in the morning, the first thing you do is skim all the headlines on the front page. (Or, if you read a tabloid, skim all the headlines of the first four or five pages.)

What you are trying to achieve here-with this first rapid, over-all view of the headlines-is "to see the world in one piece." To get a bird's-eye view of all the important events of the day at one time. *And to see, if possible, how each of these events ties in to all the others.*

For example, consider the week of March 14, 2011. Scanning the typical newspaper of any day that week, you would see that the US and European forces are supporting anti-Gadhaffi rebels in Libya ... that the threat of nuclear meltdown in Japan is not over yet ... that anti-government protests are continuing in Oman, Bahrain, Kuwait and Saudi Arabia ... Economic aftershocks of the devastation in Japan are rolling through Asia... that Belmont University's hopes of returning to the NCAA Sweet 16 were dashed by Wisconsin.

Now, what does this bird's-eye view show you? First of all-change! Country after country is changing internally. And the balance of power of the world and the environment itself is changing externally. *But exactly how? How rapidly? Towards what?*

How do these events tie in to each other? What is the connection between unrest in the middle east and the disaster in Japan? What effect will both these events have on the global economy?

This first two-minute glance tells you what happened on that day, and leads you to set up questions in your mind about why it happened, and what effect one event will have on the other.

You now read to answer these questions. You do it in this way:

HOW TO READ A NEWS STORY

2. Now you start on the articles themselves. Your objective here is to get the big facts-the important factsout of each story as fast as you can, without missing a single vital detail.

You do this by going back to the headline, and turning it into a series of questions. For example:

*US AND EUROPEAN FORCES ARE SUPPORTING
ANTI-GADHAFFI REBELS IN LIBYA*

brings these questions to mind:
> Why?
> How?
> By whom?
> What was done with him?
> *What will happen next?*

Or this headline:

THREAT OF NUCLEAR MELTDOWN IN JAPAN

brings these questions to mind:
> How big is the problem?
> How powerful would the radiation be?

How many other countries would it effect?

Does Japan have the capabilities to contain and fix the problem?

What will happen next?

Now – with these questions in mind – read the first paragraph of the story. This first paragraph is actually a complete summary of the story. It gives you an outline of what follows. It should answer most of your questions – along with Who? . . . What? . . . When? . . . Where? . . . Why? . . and How?

Now, in most stories, this first (or second, or third) paragraph should give you as much information as you want to know. In other words, it should answer your questions – at least in outline form.

However, if you wish to gain more information on any one of these points, read on. Each of the paragraphs that follow should be an expansion of one of the main points summarized in the first paragraph. You skim each paragraph till you find that point mentioned again, and then read it carefully to pick up the details you want. This way, there is no waste reading, and no waste time.

You simply:

1. Read the headline.
2. Frame the questions, you want answered about the details in that story.
3. Read the first one or two paragraphs to answer those questions.
4. And then read on only to pick up details on those points which vitally interest you.

By using this system you can get the guts of a story in a minute or two. And then you're ready to go on and

LEARN THE BACKGROUND BEHIND THE NEWS

Now – when you've read the important news of the day, and its important details – you now turn to the sections of your paper that tell you:

What does it all mean?

Now you get the comment of skilled interpreters to unravel this news and help you with your own opinions. So you next read the columnists whose job it is to assign meanings to these events.

And then you turn to the editorial pages where the paper itself interprets the news and takes stands on the major issues of the day. And where readers like yourself air their reactions in their letters to the editors.

Now – how do you pull out the gist of these many interpretations in only a few minutes each day? By reading them like this:

An editorial is built up differently from a news story. In a news story the conclusion comes first; the details later. In an editorial, however, the writer begins by reciting facts you already know – by reviewing the situation to make it fresh in your mind. And then he goes on to state his own conclusion. Or solution. Or what he wants you to think and do.

So you read a column or editorial backwards. You read the last paragraph first, to see if you can't pick up his interpretation. Then you jump to the front. Skim rapidly through the first paragraphs. Look only for background facts that you don't know ... reasons to support his interpretation ... what he thinks will happen next.

Only a few minutes for each column, and you're through with the main news of the day. But look what you've accomplished! *You've not only got the facts down solid, but you've formed your own opinions, and you've got plenty of good, solid, clearly-thought-through ideas to back them up!*

With this technique, you'll never be at sea in a serious discussion again. You.'ll know exactly where you stand on important issues. You'll think straight on crucial decisions -be able to vote more intelligently-lead other's opinions on issue after issue.

AND NOW GO ON TO FINISH THE PAPER

4. Now tum to the index. Review the minor stories. Pick out the subjects of special interest to you-sports, business, fashion, home, what have you. Use the same headline-question-answer technique on each story you glance at. Pull out the facts you want-in minutes.

If you read movie or stage or book reviews, use the same last-paragraph-first technique that you use on the editorials. Get the conclusion first. Then fill in whatever details interest you.

5· And when you're through with the paper, just don't throw it away and forget it. Think of the news as a continued story. Follow each story as it develops day by day. *Always try to anticipate what will happen next.*

6. If you can, read at least two different papers a day. Try to get different viewpoints in each. Compare them. Find out where they differ. Sharpen your reasoning power. Judge for yourself which one is right.

7. And, of course, supplement your papers with radio, TV, lectures, books, etc.

Let's see how you put one of these "bonus media" to work – in half the time you're using today.

HOW TO FLASH-READ MAGAZINES

With magazines, your plan of attack is different. Here's how to read them most efficiently:

1. Start with the Table of Contents. Check off the articles that interest you most. Turn their titles into questions, and then turn to them.

2. Read each article's tide and subtitle ... the first paragraph ... all subheads . . . and the last paragraph or two. This should give you the main idea, and enough information to tell you whether you want to read further or not.

3. If you do go further, again ask questions before you read word by word. Remember – magazines present more than mere fact; they also give you opinion. So, if you come across this kind of headline:

A PLAN TO FREE CUBA

> Ask yourself these questions:
> What is it?
> Who is its author?
> How qualified is he?
> What steps does his plan require?
> How long would it take?
> What are its chances of success?
> What would happen if it succeeded?

4. Also, remember that most magazine articles are trying to get you to feel, believe, or do something. Therefore, ask yourself:

> What reaction does this author want from me?
> How does he try to convince me that I should do this?
> What facts or arguments does he use to do this?
> What facts does he distort?
> What facts does he leave out?
> Where can I get the other side of this proposal?

5. To help you answer that last question, try to read at least two magazines-with as contrasting viewpOints as possible. Compare their interpretations. See what facts one leaves out that the other stressed. Form your own judgments.

6. Now skim through the article. Skip details. Get the main thoughts. Go on till you've answered your questions. And then turn to the next article.

7. When you've finished your main articles of interest, then quickly skim through the magazine, page by page. You may pick up something of interest that wasn't fully disclosed in the Table of Contents.

8. To read fiction in magazines, as in books, follow these rules:

HOW TO READ FICTION TWICE AS FAST, AND REMEMBER TWICE AS MUCH

1. Remember - all fiction *is about people*. Therefore, your first job is to get acquainted with the people in your book. Ask yourself: Who is the hero? Write his name on the front cover of the book. Describe him - his appearance and his character.

Who is the heroine? Write her name. Describe her. Jot down the character traits and desires that are going to determine her actions throughout the book.

Who is the villain? Describe him. List his motives. Tell why they're going to bring him in conflict with the hero.

Where are they all? Make sure you know the time and location of their surroundings.

What are they trying to do? What blocks them from doing it? *What's going to happen next?*

2. Read the first chapters carefully. They set the stage – forecast the ultimate outcome. Then read faster and faster as the characters become more familiar – as the action be comes more predictable.

3. Try to outguess the author. He's planted hints on what's going to happen at the end. Can you predict that end before he tells it to you? If you can, you'll not only get a tremendous kick out of it, but you'll learn how to see into people – predict what they'll do under stress. And this is the great benefit you're looking for from great fiction.

4. When you reach the end, ask: What happened? To whom? How did they change – for better or for worse? What is the author trying to say? What moral is he pointing out? What kind of world does he say it is? Is it true to life? Do you believe in his characters – in his events – in his outcome? This is the ultimate test.

When you've answered this question, you've told yourself whether you've just read great fiction, or pulp fiction.

And finally, what have you learned? What has this man, in this book, taught you about the way human beings act, feel, believe, fight, love, build and even die!

Never fool yourself. You can learn easily as much from fiction as you can from fact. And you can put these new in sights… these new emotions… these new competencies in handling people – to work for you, the very same day!

5. Now read the reviews. Compare their judgments with yours. Search for the *reasons* these reviewers give for their judgments. Then see if your reasons hold up as well. If not, revise and strengthen them.

6. And now turn to the back cover of the book. Sum it up in one paragraph. Who did what – against what ob stacles – and with what results? Try to boil down the entire experience – the entire moral – into one brief summary that will unlock the entire book for you again if you come back to it even a year later.

AND NOW TO CUT YOUR BUSINESS READING IN HALF

Business reading falls into two main divisions – each of which has its own problems and its own techniques. These are:

1. Keeping up with your field.

2. Plowing through a desk full of correspondence, memos, reports and what-have-you every day.

Let's take correspondence and the rest first. Here's how to lick it:

1. When you pick up a business letter, first glance at the letterhead – then immediately at the signature. (If it's a memo, look at the origin and content information at the top.) Ask yourself these questions:

Who sent it to you?

Do you know him? Do you know his company?

What do you think he wants?

What did you say in your last letter to him?

What did you want him to reply?

2. Now sweep down the letter with a glance. Most letters are usually very simple. They deal with one, two or three things. Can you see at a glance what they are? What the writer wants you to do?

3. Now read the last paragraph first. The information you want – what the writer wants you to do – should be summarized in that last paragraph.

4. Glance only briefly at the first paragraphs. They're usually filled with mere formalities ("We have your letter of the . ^. Thank you for . . . We note with great pleasure . . . etc.") Skip them. Get to the heart of the matter fast.

5. Concentrate your attention at mid-page. Here are the reasons why... the specific step-by-step that he wants done . . . the statements on which you'll have to base your decision with regard to this letter.

6. Now you can tell these facts about the letter: Is it important? If not, glance briefly through the rest, and get rid of it.

Is it your department? If not, send it to the person whose job it is.

Does it demand an answer? If so, answer it there and then, so you won't have to read it twice.

Does it demand action? If so, delegate it immediately. Get it started at once.

7. In reading memos and reports, read them backwards. Look first at the point of origin and the man who wrote it. Then look immediately at the last page. See if it's summarized. This tells you whether it's worth your time, belongs to your department, has to be read thoroughly – or whether you can simply pick up the core of it from the summary and then pass it along to someone else.

READING BUSINESS ARTICLES AND TECHNICAL REPORTS

Business articles and technical reports have three main purposes:

To report on work in progress.

To detail particulars of some specific operation or method.

To describe new and modern approaches to the problems of the profession or field.

Therefore, to keep up with your field with the least possible expenditure of time, you read them this way:

1. With a business journal, you follow the same first step as you did when reading any other kind of magazine.

Read the Table of Contents first. Mark the articles of interest. Read their summaries. Then decide if you'll read them thoroughly.

2. In reading a technical report, always define your purpose first. Tell yourself exactly why you're reading it. Exactly what you're looking for. Then disregard every thing else.

3. Don't be fooled by their formidable appearance. Their organization is usually quite simple. Read the title. Then look for a summary – usually in the first paragraphs or the last.

4. Disregard footnotes. In nine cases out of ten, they're only for specialists.

5. Concentrate on getting the main ideas. Number them. If the report describes a new procedure, look for each important step. Number them.

6. You should be able to boil down each report, each article, into a main-idea summary no longer than an index card. (If you want to keep the details, then save the article. File it with reference to the index card.)

After you've boiled it down, turn the index card over and try to repeat its contents to yourself from memory. Try to get every numbered point in the proper sequence. This gives you a stronger grip on the article's organization burns its main points into your memory.

7. *Now decide what to do with that information.* Put it to work. Use it. Adapt it. Pass it on to others so they can understand you better when you call on them to back you up. Don't just file it and forget it. New information means new ability – new power – new competence. In the long run – if it's put to use – it means new prestige and new money!

In summary:

You can double the amount of reading you get done every day – and remember twice as much of it – if you follow these simple rules:

1. *Look before you leap.* Get the main idea first. Don't start reading word-by-word till you know it.

2. *Ask questions.* Read to answer them. Stop reading when you've got their answers.

3. *Skip details.* They'll only confuse you while you're reading – slip out of your mind as soon as you close the page. Concentrate on the core. Number it. Memorize it.

4. *Then put it to work.* Remember – new knowledge means new opportunity.

CHAPTER 13

THE ALL-IMPORTANT ART OF LISTENING – RIGHT DOWN TO READING THE SPEAKER'S THOUGHTS

In addition to reading, you gain the information you need by listening. In fact, in the business and social worlds, your ability to listen well is even more important than your ability to read well. Most people gain about 80 per cent of all new facts through theil' ears, not their eyes.

Therefore hearing everything that is said, and missing nothing, is an indispensable art. But it is an art. It is not a natural gift. You must teach it to yourself. Just as you must learn how to read, so you must learn how to listen in this simple but tremendously powerful way:

HOW TO DEVELOP YOUR LISTENING POWER IN A FEW MINUTES EVERY NIGHT

When do you start to develop this ability to listen with the power of a tape recorder?

Start this way. Some night at the dinner table make up a new game for the family. Ask someone to read you a list of objects, cars, baseball players, the names of his friends, what have you. Then try to name back that list in the order in which they gave it to you.

It's as simple as that. Start with a list of ten objects.

Compete with your family. Award prizes. See how many you can name, and how much you can improve. At first you'll remember six or seven. Then eight or nine. Then all ten-perfectly.

As you go along, make the game harder. Have some one tell you a story, and repeat the important facts. Then a newspaper article. Ask them to try to stick you with specific names and figures. Watch yourself repeat them back, number by number.

You'll be astounded at how much you can retain. And how you've learned the first secret of good listening – strengthening your ear-channel memory – learning to remember everything important that you hear.

Now you're ready for the second step.

HOW TO CONCENTRATE ON THE SPEAKER'S THOUGHTS, AND NEVER BE DISTRACTED

Once you have strengthened your listening memory, so that you can hold entire thoughts and sentences in your mind after hearing them only once, you're ready to fit them together into meaningful patterns as the speaker talks. There is a definite technique to re-creating the core of a lecture or conversation – any lecture or conversation – so that you need never forget it. Here's how:

Learning to listen well – to hear everything of real importance that's being said – is primarily a matter of being able to *maintain attention*. Of pacing yourself to follow the speaker's thoughts, and not letting your mind wander off. Because of this fact, the power of complete attention has been called the mark of an educated man.

Why is it difficult to maintain this attention? Because the human brain thinks about four times as fast as the human tongue can speak. And the huge gap between the speed of your mind and the words you are hearing provides time for all sorts of distracting personal thoughts.

How do you keep these distracting thoughts from leading you astray? *By forcing yourself to keep pace with the speaker in these three ways, every time you find your mind about to wander:*

1. *By summarizing what the speaker has already said, and building it into a main-thought outline.* Here you ask yourself questions like these:

How can I sum up these statements in a single phrase?

How do they tie in with his last point?

2. *By anticipating the speaker's next point,* with questions like these:

What is he getting at here?

Where will he go now?

What examples must he give to prove this point?

3. *By listening "between the lines" for points that are not put into words,* with questions like these:

What is he implying here?

Why does he stick to this one point, and not go on to the other we were discussing last week?

Is he hinting at more than he's willing to say right out?

And so on, with other questions that will come to your mind as you seek the inner meaning of the speaker's words.

All these questions have one vital trait in common. *They turn listening from a passive to an active pursuit.* They stop drifting. They force you to think step by step with the speaker. To keep your mind constantly focused on that speaker's thoughts, both expressed and unexpressed. To literally pull the core meaning out of that lecture as it develops in front of you.

And then, as you do in your reading, night after night, you store that core meaning on paper so you can have it for good. In this way:

HOW TO TAKE LECTURE NOTES

You now have two powerful tools that enable you to capture the inner meaning of any spoken statement, lecture or conversation you may hear.

You have developed a strong listening memory, so you can hold entire thoughts and sentences in your mind after hearing them only once. And you have the ability to keep your attention focused on the speaker's thoughts, both expressed and unexpressed, for as long as necessary to pull out the inner meaning of those thoughts as it develops in front of you.

In your formal education, you now make these two gifts even more effective by learning how to re-create the backbone meaning of any lecture you may attend – in your own notebook, where you will have it for instant reference whenever you need it.

Because a word is spoken once and then is lost forever, lecture notes are prepared differently from reading notes. Though the end result is the same, the technique of capturing the main thoughts must work far faster in the lecture hall, for example, than in the reading room.

Here is that technique, step by step:

1. The more you know about the material covered by a lecture, the more you will get out of that lecture. Therefore always read the material in the textbook *before* it's covered in the lecture. Then you can use at least part of the lecture as a review, rather than a new learning experience.

2. What you are looking for in such a lecture is enrichment. This is the material that the teacher includes in his lecture that is *not* in the textbook, and that can never be picked up by mere textbook reading alone. This bonus information should form the core of the lecture, and should be what you bring home in your notebook.

3. The lecture pages in your notebook should be separate from your reading pages. To begin with, of course, you will take your lecture notes on a piece

of scrap paper, where you can jot down ideas as they seem important to you, and cross them out or rearrange them as you see corrections are necessary. Only after the lecture is over will you write them up in finished form and put them into your notebook, as we explain below.

4. These lecture notes begin the moment you walk into the room. You have already reviewed the textbook material you believe will be covered in the lecture; you are prepared to listen. Take a seat as far forward in the room as possible. Place your book and notebook on the floor, leaving on the desk only a piece of scrap paper and pen or pencil with which to write.

5. Write at the top of that paper the date, the name of the lecturer (if it is different from your regular teacher), and the subject of the lecture as soon as it is announced.

6. Your first goal is to discover the central theme, the main point, the speaker's goal in giving the lecture. You find this out in one of several ways:

It may be contained in the lecture title. A lecture on *The Five Roads to Cost Reduction,* for example, would give you the theme immediately.

If the title is vague, however, then you must look else where. Perhaps the lecturer distributes notes on mimeographed sheets before the lecture. These should be care fully read and the main thoughts underlined. If the central theme is given on the sheet, it should be transferred to your note paper immediately.

If there are no printed notes, then you must listen carefully to the lecturer's opening remarks. You should, of course, disregard introductory acknowledgments, anecdotes, jokes, and so on, and concentrate on picking up such signal phrases as the following:

"I wish to discuss tonight the problem of – "
"The theme of my lecture tonight will be – "
"Have you ever thought of the extreme importance of this country of – "

Somewhere in these opening remarks, the main theme will emerge. As soon as you have it, it should be boiled down in your mind to one or two phrases, and written at the top of your paper. There it will control the development of your outline – tell you exactly what to look for in the rest of the lecture.

HOW TO RECOGNIZE THE SPEAKER'S MAIN POINTS

7. Once you know the main theme of the lecture, your next goal is obvious. You must chart the development of that central theme through one vital thought after another. You are now building your outline from the speaker's words – listening for main thoughts and writing each of them down in order.

99

8. To do this you listen 90 percent of the time and write the other ten. Note taking is not stenography. It is never merely writing down the exact words the lecturer uses, even if that were possible. Note taking is condensation. Judgment. Weeding out the unimportant. Boiling down the central thoughts, as they occur, to a few capsule words or phrases, and then fitting them into their place in your growing outline.

9. How do you recognize these main thoughts? In two ways. First because they are big ideas pertaining to the central theme of the lecture. (For example, in a lecture on *The Five Roads to Cost Reduction,* once you have heard the speaker say, *"Now, the first road to cost reduction is, of course, to cut raw materials costs,"* you would know that you had your first main thought.

10. Next, you recognize the lecture's main thoughts by the *signal words* the speaker uses to introduce them. These signal words are much like the chapter signposts that guided you to the meaning of your textbook reading. They are verbal signals that flag your attention, that warn you that something really important will follow them. Let's look at a few of them right now.

Any number is a direct give-away that the speaker is going to list his main points for the audience. He may even give the audience advance notice of how many main points he's going to have, in this way:

"Now, the geographical setting of ancient Greece had three main influences upon Greek civilization."

At that point you mark in your rough notes:

Influences of geographical setting:

1. ....
....
2. ....
....
3. ....
....

You now know that there are three geographical influences, and you have set aside space for each of the three as they come up in the lecture. You now have a built-in *main-thought trap* in your notes. Listen without writing until the speaker signals again, by saying: *"The first geographical influence- "*

Then write it down, and wait for the second and the third.

These number signals are the most clear-cut clues the speaker will give to the number and arrangement of his main thoughts. But there are others almost as useful. Here are some of them, and what they tell you. That another important fact is coming-next, then, further, besides, moreover, but, in addition.

That another important event is taking place in the speaker's time sequence – *then, soon, meanwhile, later, at last, finally.*

That the speaker is going to illustrate a main point by a specific case – *for example, especially, in particular.*

That a new main point is going to be introduced to contrast with the main point that has just been covered – *on the other hand, yet, still, however, on the contrary, but, nevertheless.*

That the lecture is coming to a conclusion (at this point watch for a summing up that will give you a chance to check and see whether you have all the main points in their right order) – *in conclusion, to sum up, finally, hence, so, thus, as a result.*

And, finally, other signal words to watch for, because they may point up a main thought that follows them, are – *all things considered, above all, for this reason, to this end, likewise, and so.*

HOW THE LECTURER POINTS OUT THE QUESTIONS HE'S GOING TO ASK ON FUTURE TESTS

11. In addition to these automatic signal words that point out the main thoughts of the lecture, the speaker many times will deliberately pause, then tell the class that such and such a point is going to be asked for in a future test. He may use any one of the following forms to announce this:

"It is important to note – "
"Be sure to know – "
"Pay special attention to – "
Or he may come right out and say it:
"You'll be asked to – "
"This will be a test question – "

Once you hear these clues, set this point off from the rest of the lecture in this way. Mark a large TQ (for Test Question) beside it. Then, in your review later on, you can give it special attention.

HOW TO FINISH THE NOTES SO THEY CONTAIN EVERYTHING YOU NEED FROM THE LECTURE

12. Now what have you done so far during this lecture? You have: written down the central theme at the top of your paper. jotted down the main headings as they were either out lined at the beginning of the lecture, or as they emerged during its development, left plenty of room after each of these headings to serve as main-thought traps to pick up their vital sub-points, and filtered out these sub-points by careful, active listen ing, and by following the clues the speaker's signal words gave you.

13. Therefore, at the end of the lecture, you should have the main-thought backbone of that lecture completely down on your rough sheet of paper. *Now your job is to rewrite those notes into finished form as soon as possible.*

14. If you have the time, stay in the lecture hall after the others have left, and rewrite them there. Use the first available five minutes to fix those notes firmly in your note book and in your mind.

15. Rewrite them in this way. Reread everything you have put down on the rough sheet of paper, making sure you understand each point and its relation to every other point in the lecture. Then, if necessary, put them in the correct and final order. Weed out. Number. Underscore. Organize. Until you have these notes written as clearly and completely as your reading notes every night.

16. This is your first self-recitation of the material in this lecture. When you have finished it, and when you have fitted it into place behind your other lecture notes, you have made that lecture your own. You are now ready to relate it to your reading notes on the same material, and put it to use whenever you need it for a test.

TWO OTHER VITAL CLASSROOM TECHNIQUES

At one time or another during a lecture, no matter how bright you are, you will have a moment when you just don't understand one of the speaker's statements, or when you have a thought that would modify that statement. Therefore you must get into the habit of asking questions, of speaking up in the classroom.

If the teacher allows questions during the lecture, ask a brief, polite, to-the-point question immediately. This question should have one purpose: to clear up the point that is vague in your mind. Once it is cleared up, write the point and its answer in your rough notes, and check it later to make sure you have understood it. As we shall discuss later, any misunderstanding is a golden opportunity for learning.

If the teacher does not permit questions during the lecture, then speak to him after class. In any case, never leave the classroom with the question unanswered.

At the same time, if sample problems are done by the teacher during the lecture, copy them, word by word, right into your notebook.

This is essential – especially in your mathematics classes – for these two reasons:

First, because it trains you away from attempting your own short-cut methods, where you may leave out vital steps and get hopelessly lost. And it eliminates the necessity for you to copy answers rather than mastering the methods that produce them.

When you start to apply problem-solving techniques, there will be no pat answers to copy. Then only methods will be of any use. (And, if you are going to compete, you had darned well better know them.)

And secondly, this step-by-step copying of sample problems is one more way of assuring attentiveness. Again, the best way by far to learn is actively, with a pencil in your hand.

In summary:

Power-listening can be developed as effectively as Power-reading, simply by learning a few easy techniques. These are:

Strengthening your listening memory, so you can retain whole phrases, thoughts, and sentences in your mind after hearing them only once.

Teaching yourself to maintain full concentrated atterrtion on the speaker's words, so that no important thought, expressed or unexpressed, can escape you.

And learning how to boil a lecture down into its vital thoughts, each in its proper order, so you can store the backbone meaning of that lecture in your mind and your notebook for instant reference whenever you need it.

PART THREE

EXPRESSING THE FACTS –
WRITING AND CONVERSING

CHAPTER 14

THE FIRST ESSENTIAL –
CORRECT SPELLING MADE EASY

In your day-to-day life, when you are submitting a resume for an important job, or writing an application for membership in a club, *a single mistake in spelling* can ruin the entire impression you are trying to make. And yes, there will be times when a computer and spell check are not available...

You cannot afford to be satisfied with anything less in your spelling than 100 percent perfect. And it can be, if you follow these simple rules:

THE WRONG AND RIGHT WAYS
TO IMPROVE YOUR SPELLING

In the first place, *don't* try to improve your spelling by going over lists of misspelled words and trying to correct them. These lists only concentrate your attention on the wrong spelling.

Instead, focus your efforts on the *right spelling,* in the right way, like this:

Realize that the reason you misspell any word is because you have a *distorted* image of that word in your mind. Your job is to get rid of that distorted image, and replace it with the correct one in such a way that it is burned forever into your memory.

You do this in three simple steps:

First, you see that word in such a way that the *correct spelling* of the hard part of the word sticks out like a sore thumb.

Second, you learn simple *spell-alikes* for the hard part of the word that brings the right spelling of it automatically to your mind every time.

And third, you write that word *twice as large as you ordinarily write,* until you get the correct *feel* of the word forever implanted in the muscles of your arm.

Not only are these three correction steps simple and easy, they are also enormous fun. Let's see how each of them works:

STEP ONE: SEE THE HARD PART OF THE WORD CORRECTLY

As you know, most words that are misspelled are misspelled in only one place in the entire word. Either you have added a letter where it shouldn't be, or forgotten one where it should be, or put in an *e* for an *a*, or doubled a letter when it should remain single, or some other simple mistake.

But, once you have developed that distorted image of the word, then it sticks in your mind. You misspell that word over and over again, always in the same way, always in the same place.

From that moment on, there is a part of that word that you automatically misspell. It is that *hard part* on which you now concentrate.

First, you check over your writing and pick out the misspelled words. Then you locate the hard part of each of those words – the one or two letters in it that you automatically misspell.

And then you rewrite that word correctly – this time CAPITALIZING those hard letters.

You write it like this:
>   climB
>   boRRow
>   UNable
>   paraLLel
>   tomoRRow
>   arGUMent, and so on.

Now, copy this correct spelling on a second sheet of paper – over and over again – *with the capitals in exactly the same place that you have put them.*

Write that word over and over and over again – capitals and all – until you've got it down pat. Until you can see the correct capitalized spelling of the hard part of that word *with your eyes shut.*

Then you've completed your first step. You're well on your way to perfect spelling.

STEP TWO: BUILD AN AUTOMATIC MEMORY PROMPTER TO SPELL THE HARD PART OF THE WORD CORRECTLY

Now, you are going to reinforce that correct picture image of that word in your mind. You are going to do it by creating a simple *spell-alike* to help you remember how the difficult letters go.

You are going to create an *automatic memory tie-in* between the difficult part of the word and an easy-to-remember spell-alike, like this:

There are three different ways to create these spellalikes. Try them in the following order, until you get one that you automatically remember.

First of all, look for *familiar words within the hard words,* to make them easy to remember. Make up little sentences that tie these familiar words and the hard words together. For example:

"The SECRET was kept by the SECRETary."
"After I ATE, I was grATEful."
"We will GAIN a barGAIN."
"It's VILE to allow special priVILEge."
"Scientists LABOR in a LABORatory."

Second, if there are no familiar words within the hard words, then look for the *same part* in smaller familiar words.

For example:

"We write a lettER on our stationERy."
"When we PARt, we sePARate."
"Please BRing the umBRella."

Finally, if neither of these first two rules works, then make up pure spell-alikes-as funny and as nonsensical as possible. For example:

"She screamed EEE as she passed the cEmEtEry."
"The RR train and I had a quaRRel."
"GM uses good judGMent."
"I gave HER HER handKERchief."
"I say BR when I think of FeBRuary."

There is a spell-alike for every misspelled word. One of these three rules will tum up the right one for you. Remember, keep them as vivid and as funny as possible; in that way, they'll be much easier to remember.

And, once you're on to the game, let the whole family think up the spell-alikes. It's not only great fun to see who can come up with the most outlandish ones, but it's marvelous training for future creativity.

And, always, it makes the correct spelling of those difficult words *automatic*, as soon as the spell-alike flashes into your mind to tell you the way those hard letters should go.

STEP THREE: GET THE ARM-FEEL OF WRITING
THAT HARD WORD CORRECTLY

Now, after you've capitalized the hard part of that misspelled word, and after you've thought up a spell-alike to remember its correct order automatically, then you are ready to *build the correct spelling of the word into a written reflex* without even thinking of it.

Here's how:

Take a piece of blank, unruled paper. Write the word in natural script, without the capital letters, across the top of the paper. But this time write it TWICE AS BIG as you ordinarily would.

TWICE AS BIG, over and over and over again. Write it without looking at it. Never hesitate. Never stop in the middle. If you get the word wrong, run through the first two steps again. And then go back to the TWICE AS BIG writing immediately.

Over and over again. Until you build the writing of that word into a mechanically perfect skill. Until you get the word down letter-perfect. Until you can write it correctly as casually as you write your own signature.

Then it belongs to you. You have it – forever.

HOW TO MAKE THIS THREE-STEP SYSTEM
WORK FOR YOU EVERY DAY!

To learn a new word, as we have said before, means to know its meaning, its use in a sentence, its correct pronun ciation, and its correct spelling. Until all these are letterperfect, you really don't own the word at all.

As you advance through your business and social life, you will meet more and more important new words. Some of them you will mispell. Therefore you should have a Spelling Section in the back of your notebook or journal. I suggest that you keep this Spelling Section for your reading notes and/or home-study courses.

Divide this Section into two parts. Title the first part "Misspelled Words," and mark down in it any word you misspell.

Every night take one of these misspelled words – no more – and use the system to teach yourself its correct spelling.

Then when you have had that word letter-perfect, list it in the second part of the Spelling Section under the title "Mastered Words."

When you have listed about ten or twelve of these mastered words, have someone dictate all of them to you in a short paragraph or story. Then check each of their spellings.

If any are misspelled, put them back in the first part of the Section, and start all over again, because you haven't established the correct habit yet.

But you will. Before you know it, you'll be amazed at the absolute precision you show in these spelling tests. And once you have mastered a word, use it as often as possible. This will help you practice, to keep the correct spelling fresh in your mind. It will also build confidence -show you over and over again that you no longer have the slightest reason to be afraid of misspelling that once terrifying word.

In summary:

There's only one permissible way to spell; that is 100 percent, letter-perfect.

This can be easily done if you correct every spelling error, individually, with this simple three-step method:

1. Detect the one or two letters in each difficult word that you automatically spell wrong. Then CAPITALIZE the correct spelling of those letters till they stick out in front of your eyes like a sore thumb.

2. Think up spell-alikes for the hard letters that auto matically remind you of the correct way those hard letters should go.

3. And then get the feel of hand spelling the word right, over and over and over again, twice as big as life, till you jot it down correctly as easily and as automatically as you write your name.

This three-step system, applied daily to master one mis spelled word, will make you a spelling whiz in far less time than you believed possible.

And now we turn to your ability to express thoughts on paper – professional writing secrets that will enable you to turn in top-grade letters, memos, speeches, sales presentations, reports and what-have-you – almost as fast as the words can form in your mind.

CHAPTER 15

HOW TO WRITE AS EASILY AND QUICKLY
AS YOU THINK

The farther you advance in the business and social world, the more you will be required to prepare resumes, interoffice memos, engineering reports, business and social letters, club minutes, and much, much more. .

All of this vital work will be written. All of it will require that you be able to set down your thoughts, suggestions, goals on paper-so clearly and so persuasively that those papers serve as your best salesmen.

Therefore, the ability to write well is equally as important to you as the ability to speak well. You must be as fluid with your pen as you are with your tongue. You must be just as much at home writing a technical report as you are telling a friend about a ball game.

You must develop *ease in writing*.

Ease in writing, and precision in writing, come from two sources, both of which are available to you.

    1. *Practice* and
    2. *Planning*

It is the combination of these two that constitute power writing. Let us see how you can build both of them into your every written word, and HOW YOU CAN DISCOVER EXACTLY WHAT TO WRITE FROM THE BEGINNING TO THE END OF EVERY PAPER.

Like reading, and perhaps even more so, writing demands a plan of attack, a definite goal that you want to achieve in every composition, and a definite plan to get there. A series of questions that puts you immediately on the right road, and keeps you there from the first word you write to the last.

Let's look at such a series of direction questions right now. Let's work out a typical idea – for example, a paper you might prepare for a magazine article, or a speech before your club – and see how these questions and answers avoid errors, strengthen the power of what you have to say and cut your writing time in half.

Let's take as our subject *Should America Pull Its Troops Out of Afghanistan?* Let's assume that you answer the question with a "Yes," that America should pull its troops out, and see how you develop the subject.

First of all, you should ask yourself these questions:

What exactly am I going to write about in this paper? (About whether America should pull its troops out of Afghanistan.)

Can I express this key idea in a single sentence, before I begin to write? (Yes. America should should pull its troops out.)

How much am I going to say about it? (I'm going to list the reasons why America should pull its troops.)

What am I NOT going to say about it, because I don't have the room? (Two things: (1) I am not going to list any arguments for the other side, why America should not pull its troops; and (2) I am not going to discuss any of the political problems that we'll have to overcome.)

What specific points am I going to make about this idea? (The specific reasons why we should be first: Because it will help our image with the other Arab nations. Because they no longer want us there. Becasue it will save the lives of our young men and women in the Armed Forces. Because it will reduce the economic deficit spent on maintaining the troops over there. And because of the lack of NATO/European support.)

How many of these points are there? (Five.)

In what order should they be arranged? Which should come first, second, third, and so on? (In this order: First, save lives; second, reduce spending; third, no longer wanted there; fourth, other Arab nations; and fifth, lack of NATO/European support.

Which of these points are the most important; which should be given separate paragraphs? (All of them.)

Which points should I group into one paragraph? (None.)

What is the best way to catch my reader's interest? (Probably with strong, emphatic assertion at the very beginning. Something like this: "There are at least five vital reasons why America should pull its troops out of Afghanistan, anyone of which would more than justify this move.")

How do I end? Can I think of a good last sentence before I begin to write? (Yes. A summary sentence something like this: "Therefore, to reduce our casualities, to strengthen our own economy, to maintain our prestige with the uncommitted nations of the world, and because we are not wanted there, it is essential that we pull our troops from Afghanistan.")

HOW YOU PERFECT YOUR COMPOSITION BEFORE YOU BEGIN TO WRITE IT

The questions outlined above give you two major benefits. They force you to choose a definite, easily handled topic, clearly formulated, concrete and specific, with no chance of wandering over its chosen limits. And they help you write about this topic one step at a time, with each step in its proper place.

Without such a blueprint, you simply won't know where you're going, and revising your paper will take you more time than originally writing it.

Now, once you have the answers to these questions, arrange them quickly in a Main Thought Outline, just as you do in your daily reading. The process in both reading and writing is the same, but it is done in the reverse. In writing, you get main thoughts first, build them into an outline second, and then write the paper itself on the basis of that outline.

Here is how you build that outline.

Write your title for the paper across the top of the out line: *"Why America Should Should Pull Its Troops Out Of Afghanistan."*

Write the first sentence directly below this title: *"There are at least five vital reasons why America should pull its troops out of Afghanistan, any one of which would more than justify this action."*

Take the first major idea and mark it with the Roman numeral I:

"I. Because it will save the lives of our young men and women in the Armed Forces."

If this first major idea demands more than one paragraph to explain it fully, then mark each one of these paragraphs with the capital letters A, B, C, and so on:

   "A. The death rate is steadily increasing."

   "B. The risk is too high."

   "C. Our troops are not properly equipped."

Each of these paragraphs will have several sentences within it, to develop important details. These detail sentences are marked in the outline by Arabic numerals, and are placed under the capital letter paragraph to which they belong. For example, in paragraph A above, you would have these detail sentences:

"A. The death rate is steadily increasing"

    1. We are now facing casualties from supposed friendlies.

    2. Roadside bombs.

    3. Suicide bombers.

    4. No clear battle lines.

Continue on, developing every major idea in this way, marking them with the Roman numerals II, III, IV, and so on. Then breaking them into their separate paragraphs, and marking these with the capital letters, A, B, C, and so on. Then outlining the individual detail-sentences with Arabic numerals 1, 2, 3, and so on, till you have finished outlining the entire paper.

You then write in your concluding sentence, and you are finished with the outline. Here is a brief sample of what that outline will look like at that stage:

WHY AMERICA SHOULD PULL ITS TROOPS OUT OF AFGHANISTAN

There are at least five vital reasons why America should pull its troops out of Afghanistan, any one of which would more than justify this action:

I. Because it will save the lives of our young men and women in the Armed Forces.

    A. The death rate is steadily increasing

        1. We are now facing casualties from supposed friendlies.

        2. Roadside bombs.

        3. Suicide bombers.

        4. No clear battle lines.

    B.

        1.

        2.

        3.

    C.

        1.

        2.

        3.

II. Because it will reduce the economic deficit spent on maintaining the troops over there.

    A.

And so on, till the outline is finished.

HOW TO WRITE THE FINISHED DRAFT OF THE PAPER

From this point on, the final draft of the composition writes itself.

You take the title and the first sentence and put them down on the paper. Then take main idea I and phrase it into your next paragraph, like this:

"First of all, of course, such steps are necessary in order to protect the lives of our soldiers.

Now take each of the three paragraphs under this main idea I, and build them according to the outline, like this:

In this conflict, the death rate has been steadily increasing instead of being reduced by our presence.

This has been brought about by a number of factors including the recent attacks on training schools by supposed friendlies.

Add to that the increased risk of IEDs, Improvised Explosive Devices or roadside bombs where are a tactic being used at alarming rates, the risk of attack by suicide bomber and the fact that there are no clear battle lines and one can only come to the same conclusions.

And so on. Paragraph by paragraph, right through the entire paper.

When you are through, you will have a composition that develops your subject thoroughly, that presents your points in logical, persuasive order that makes good reading and makes sense, and that persuades other people to your point of view.

TIPS ON WRITING THAT DEVELOP CLARITY AND POWER

1. Every paragraph should contain only one main idea and the details that develop it. When you go on to discuss a second main idea, start a new paragraph.

This has been shown over and over again in the examples we have given above.

2. Each sentence, in its turn, should contain only one idea. The great mistake most poor writers make is in trying to crowd too many ideas into a single sentence. This results in huge, clumsy, poorly understood sentences. When you get to a second idea - or when you find two or more ideas crowded against each other in a single sentence - separate them and build each into its own sentence.

EXAMPLE:

WRONG WAY: *After we anived home from the trip, tired and dirty, we immediately went upstairs, where we unpacked our clothes and hung them up, before we allowed ourselves to take a shower and go to bed.*

CLEARER AND MORE POWERFUL: *We arrived home from the trip, tired and dirty. We immediately went upstairs. Yet, before we allowed ourselves to take a shower and go to bed, we unpacked our clothes and hung them up.*

3. Long sentences are usually confused sentences. One sure way to avoid this mistake, and to write clearer, stronger sentences, is to keep the subject and predicate of each sentence as close together as possible.

EXAMPLE:

WRONG WAY: *The man whom Tom had seen earlier that day running away from the bank spun around when he saw Tom.*

The subject of this sentence is "man" and its predicate is "spun." The reason the sentence is confusing is that this subject and predicate are separated so widely by the clause "whom Tom had seen earlier that day running away from the bank." Therefore, to make these two thoughts far more powerful and clear, they should be separated like this:

RIGHT WAY: *It was the man whom Tom had seen earlier that day running away from the bank. When he saw Tom again, he spun around.*

4. Make sure your sentences are connected correctly. You have to point out the relation between one sentence and the next. Otherwise, your reader won't know where your train of thought is going.

Connecting words are *and, yet, but, so, or, for, however, therefore, thus, otherwise, because, from, such, this* and so on. They point out to your reader what your second sentence has to do with your first, what your third has to do with your second, and so on.

EXAMPLES: A good exercise would be to go through a few pages of any good book and underline the connecting words the author uses. Ask yourself how each connect ing word ties in one sentence with the sentence that goes before.

This way, you will develop skill in using these tie-in words, and your papers will be a powerful procession of closely woven thoughts.

In summary:

The ability to write well is as important as the ability to speak well, and it is as easy to learn.

You should learn and practice the principles of planning from today on. Before you start to write a word you should already have defined your subject, your main thoughts, and your opening and closing sentences.

And you should have arranged them in paragraph-by-paragraph order in a Main Thought Outline, so your paper will practically write itself when you sit down to begin it.

PART FOUR

MASTERING FACTS –
THE ART OF REMEMBERING AND REVIEW

CHAPTER 16

ERRORS – THE ROYAL ROAD TO KNOWLEDGE

Every person, no matter how bright or slow he is, learns some facts quickly and has trouble with others. Those he learns easily require little outside help. It is the troublesome fact, the error-causing fact, the fact that blocks the road to understanding that we must concentrate upon.

The telltale symptom of trouble, of course, is a mistake in your work. Most people are troubled by such mistakes. *They do not realize that if they are handled correctly, they are worth their weight in gold.*

Why? Because a mistake is actually nothing more or less than a signpost in your work that identifies misunderstanding.

And by analyzing what went wrong in each of those mistakes, and correcting it, you will achieve a far deeper level of understanding and competence than you could ever gain without them.

This is perfectly in accord with the prime rule of all self-improvement – *work on weaknesses*. Your strengths you will always have. But your weaknesses must be identified and gone over and over again until they are no longer there.

Let us therefore examine this technique of turning a mistake into gold. It is as simple as this:

HOW YOU CAN PROFIT FROM YOUR MISTAKES

It is never enough for you simply to glance at a test when it is handed back to you and notice that you have made an error on it.

For every test error (or any error on any work) that you make, you must be able to answer these three questions about that error before you go on to new work:

1. Where in the problem did you make the mistake?

2. What did you do wrong that caused you to make that mistake?

3. What is the correct operation that will avoid that same kind of mistake in the future?

Let's see how these three questions turn errors into accomplishments.

STEP ONE: LOCATE THE ERROR

For example, let's say that you come up with a wrong answer in a profit and loss problem.

You know that the answer is wrong, *but where exactly did it go wrong?*

Was it a mistake in multiplication or subtraction, or addition inside the problem? Was it only one mistake or several?

To find out, break the problem down into steps. Check each step to find out which one went wrong. Don't rest till you can pinpoint the exact step where each error occurred.

STEP TWO: FIND OUT WHAT CAUSED IT:

Now, when you've located the exact spot where the error occurred, you have to identify its cause.

Let's say that it was a mistake in one of your percentages. You took a 47% mark-up on $500 worth of goods, and came up with a sales price of $745.

What caused you to make this mistake?

Was it simply carelessness? Or is that mistake a warning that you're weak in your multiplication?

STEP THREE: CORRECT THE CAUSE OF THE ERROR

If it was carelessness, review again the techniques of checking an answer to make sure its right.

If, however, you do show a weakness in multiplication, stop everything and review multiplication. Do it over and over again until it becomes automatic and automatically right.

Remember, you have to correct the *cause* of an error before you can permanently correct the error itself. If you do not correct the cause first, the error will simply repeat itself later on.

STEP FOUR: CORRECT THE ERROR ITSELF

Now take a fresh sheet of paper, copy the problem onto that paper and work it again. This time it should come out right. If it does, file it away and come back to it the following week. Try it again on a fresh piece of paper.

If you get it right again, then you can forget about it. If not, do it again. Never allow yourself to make the same mistake twice!

STEP FIVE: DO SIMILAR PROBLEMS TO MAKE SURE YOU'VE GOT THE CORRECT TECHNIQUE

At the same time, give yourself several other mark-up problems. Concentrate on them. Within a short time you'll have mastered them all, and the correct answer.

In summary:

Follow this same technique with every mistake you make.

Break the problem down into steps.

See which step went wrong.

Find out why.

Correct the cause of the error.

Work the problem the right way.

And keep doing it over and over again until the right answer is absolutely automatic.

This way mistakes help rather than harm you. You won't make that mistake , or its first cousin, again. You have removed a misunderstanding - roadblock from your mind.

This process of turning errors into achievements is one of the finest forms of *review. We now turn to a complete discussion of this all-important subiect.*

CHAPTER 17

HOW TO BURN FACTS, LESSONS, WHOLE SUBJECTS INTO YOUR MIND – FOR GOOD

We are now ready to review what you have learned so far in this book, and tie it together into one over-all plan for mastering any subject you may study. Mastering a course – any course – consists of the following logical steps:

1. Find out what it is that you have to learn in each assignment in the course.

2. Read that assignment to get at the heart of its meaning.

3. Write that core meaning down in your notebook in a few brief sentences or phrases, related to each other through the outline form.

4. Tie the outline of that assignment into the assignment that came before it.

5. *Then review as much as you have studied of the entire book or course EVERY WEEK, to get an over-all view of everything you've learned.*

6. *At the end of the term, a week or two before the final test, make a final review of your strengths and weaknesses throughout the entire course. Here you find out what you know well; what you should know better; what you really do not know at all.*

And on the basis of this final review, you create the final study schedule for the week before the test.

This, then, is your Plan of Mastery for your studies. We have already discussed Steps 1 through 4. We now turn to Steps 5 and 6 – the strategy of review, of fixing the heart of your course permanently in your mind.

WHAT REVIEW IS NOT

First of all, let us define review by saying quite definitely what it is *not*.

Review is *not* cramming, *not* last-minute effort, *not* the desperate piling up of information in frenzied disorder.

This type of cramming always fails. It always has failed. It always will fail.

Why? Because it attempts to store up large quantities of *unorganized* material. And without organization, there can be no memory. Material crammed into your brain leaks out again as fast as it goes in.

WHAT IS EFFECTIVE REVIEW?

Boiled down to its essentials, active effective reviewing is nothing more or less than this:

Continuous self-examination – of the essential parts of a course.

Effective review, then, consists of these two essential steps:

1. Boiling down the material of the course to its essentials, and then boiling the essentials down again and again and again, until you've mastered every word of the core meaning of that course.

2. Periodically reviewing that core material – through continuous self-examination – until every word of its content is right at the tip of your tongue, ready to be instantly formed into an answer.

For example, mathematics is thus reduced to rules, definitions, types of problems that will be encountered in the final test, and the formulas and procedures that will solve them. Then all this essential knowledge is rehearsed, over and over again, until the correct answer to any one of the problems becomes an automatic and instant reaction.

This is the same combination of knowledge and practice that makes a champion line backer, a top-flight golfer, or a superbly successful executive.

Once you have reviewed your course in this way – in other words, once you have reduced it to its essentials and practiced quizzing yourself on those essentials till they have become second nature – you are ready to breeze through any test that can be thrown at you on that subject.

Now, let's examine this process of review and readiness, step by step. There are three steps:

    1. Weekly review.

    2. Final organization of notebook.

    3. Final quiz-review of the entire course.

Let's look at each one:

STEP ONE: THE WEEKLY REVIEW

Effective review, of course, is not a once-a-course activity. It goes on constantly, first as part of your day-by-day study, then to survey a larger area once every week, and then to insure understanding of the entire course at the end of the term.

We have already discussed, in Chapter 10, the first step in this continuous process. On page 95, we went over the three questions you use to tie in each new chapter with the one that went before. These were:

"In one sentence, what did I learn from last night's chapter?"

"How does this tie in with the chapter before?"

"What questions will I be asked on it in next week's test?"

Now, at the end of each study week, you go one step further. Each week, you set aside one additional half hour for review of the entire book up to that point.

During this hour, you review each chapter outline in your notebook. You then tie them together – in a continuously growing over-all view of the book as a whole – with this series of questions and answers:

"How many chapters have I now read in this book?" (Using the history book as our example: Three, plus an introduction.)

"What is the title of the book?" (A History of Civilization.)

"Does this title give the theme of the book?" (It does.)

If it did not, you would then ask the question:

"What is the theme of the book?" (A history of civilization.)

"What, if any, is the title of the introduction?" ("The Uses of History.")

"What, in one sentence, is the core meaning of the introduction?" (A study of history keeps us from making the same mistakes all over again that our ancestors made.)

"What is the title of the first chapter?" ("The First Men.")

"What, in one sentence, is the core meaning of the first chapter?" (Primitive man spent almost all his time getting enough food to keep alive, until he invented agriculture.)

"What is the title of the second chapter?" ("The Near East.")

"What, in one sentence, is the core meaning of the sec ond chapter?" (The first great civilizations in history – ruled by kings and priests and resting on slavery – were built in the Near East.)

"How does the second chapter tie in with the first?" (By showing the tremendous growth in civilization agriculture made possible, even though this civilization was enjoyed only by the few who had seized rule.)

"What is the title of the third chapter?" ("The Greeks.")

"What, in one sentence, is the core meaning of the third chapter?" (The Greeks developed the first Western civilization, inventing democracy, science, philosophy, literature, and so on.)

"How does the third chapter tie in with the second?" (By showing the contrast between the older, king- and priest-dominated civilizations of the Near East, and the new freedom that characterized Greek civilization.) And so on. Chapter by chapter, every week of each course.

This never-ceasing weekly review pays off several ways. It keeps the older chapters fresh in your mind. It ties in each new chapter with all the material that preceded it. It gives you an ever-growing over-all view of the course as a unified whole. It cuts down the amount of reviewing you will need to do in the last two weeks before your final exams.

And it helps you to simplify and to bring your note book up to date, like this:

STEP TWO: THE FINAL ORGANIZATION OF YOUR NOTEBOOK

At the end of each course, when you are ready to begin your final review, you have in your notebook:

1. A main-thought outline of every textbook chapter in the course.

2. A main-thought outline of every lecture you have been given in the course.

3. If there are any, main-thought outlines of any out side reference reading you have been assigned during the course, done in the same way as any daily reading assignment.

4. A fundamental vocabulary page for the course as a whole.

5. A list of the mistakes you have made in your test papers during the progress of the course.

These five different parts of your notebook must now be brought together into a single final outline page for each chapter in the course.

They must be blended together – unified – with all the duplicate facts removed. They must be arranged in a single, logical order, so that every fact you have learned during the entire course *fits in perfectly,* and can be remembered – automatically – the instant you need it.

This final blending is done in this way:

FIRST:

For each chapter, take your reading notes and lecture notes (and, if there are any, outside reference notes) and lay them side by side.

Then take a third sheet of paper and start to blend them in, point by point. Start with the chapter title, then the first main thought underneath that title, then the second, and right on down the line.

To help you with this blending task ask yourself the following questions:

"Is this fact repeated by both sources?" If so, throw it out.

"Is this fact new?" If so, put it under the proper heading in your revised outline.

"Do I have to change the order of my headings because of any new facts?" Sometimes when material from separate sources is put together, you will find that neither of the older outlines can contain the blended facts. In this case, you must construct a brand-new outline and order containing all the new facts in their proper relation to each other.

"Are all these facts really important – are they really main thoughts – or are some of them merely details describing other main thoughts already picked up from another source?" If so, leave them out.

These questions cause you to weigh and choose and reject. They make your mind work. In themselves, they are an excellent form of review. And when you are finished answering them, and shaping their answers into a final mainthought chapter outline, you will pretty well know every thing there is to know about the material in that chapter

SECOND:

Now, go back over your lecture notes for that chapter, and ask yourself the following questions:

"What questions will I be most likely asked about this chapter?"

"What points have been stressed in classroom lectures?"

"What information were we told to pay special attention to in the textbook?"

Every time you find the answer to one of these questions in your lecture notes, place a red check in front of that point in your revised main-thought outline. This check will serve as a signal to you when you compose your final review questions, as we will describe below.

Now throw away your reading notes, lecture notes, and reference notes. You have no more need for them, since they have been blended into your revised main-thought outlines.

THIRD:

Now turn to the fundamental-vocabulary page. Remove this page from your notebook and lay it alongside your revised main-thought outlines for the course.

Go down the vocabulary, word by word, and check off the point in the main-thought outlines where that word is first used in the course. At that point, make an asterisk (*) in the main-thought outline, and then write the word and its definition at the bottom of that outline page.

Do this till you have exhausted every word you have in the fundamental vocabulary. You have then tied the vocabulary in with your notes, and gained a deeper under standing of both in doing it.

But do not throw away the fundamental-vocabulary page. Continue to carry it at the back of the notebook as an instant reference if you should forget the meaning of the words as they appear in more advanced lessons.

FOURTH:

Now take out your daily or weekly written work, and check each one of the mistakes you have made during the entire course. Wherever you have made a mistake, place a red check mark against the same point in your main-thought outlines.

This again reminds you to pay special attention to that point in your final review.

You now have a completely revised and ready-for-review notebook. It contains every fact you have learned from your reading, your lectures and your reference research, all blended together into one thoroughly understood stream of thought.

In addition, you have incorporated into those outlines probable test questions, a thorough understanding of the vocabulary of the course, and review signals for every weak spot that has shown up in your work for the entire term. You are now ready to perform one final review operation on that notebook, which will thoroughly prepare you for your final test by enabling you to anticipate 80 per cent or more of all the questions your teacher can give you, IN THE EXACT FORM THAT THAT TEACHER CAN PHRASE THEM.

STEP THREE: THE FINAL QUIZ –
REVIEW OF THE ENTIRE COURSE

Let us say that you have begun your final revision of your notebook two weeks before the final exam. It has taken you one week to complete this revision, and thus to master the main thoughts of the entire course.

You now have one week left to prepare yourself to breeze through that final exam. In the next chapter we will outline day-by-day, step-by-step procedures for that final week. Right now, however, we will see how you take your revised notes during that final week, a*nd turn them into your own private test before the real test,* to make sure you know every detail of that material.

There are two ' reasons, of course, why you take this private test before the real test:

1. Obviously, because it gives you one final chance to again review your material, to gain still deeper understanding of it, and more confidence in handling it.

2. Because it is one thing to know the core material of a course, and quite another thing to be able quickly and accurately to answer test questions about it. To really whiz through a test, you should be familiar with the questions you are going to be asked on that test – not only their form, but their very content. And the only way you can discover that content – outside of cheating – is to construct your own test out of the same materials your teacher will use to construct his.

Therefore you now begin to turn your revised notes into test questions, in this way:

HOW TO MAKE UP YOUR OWN TEST QUESTIONS

As we mentioned in Chapter 10, page 90, each page of your notes is written on one side only. You have purposely left the opposite side of those notes blank. You are now going to put that blank side to work.

Let us say that you are going to review our sample chapter 3, *The Five Roads to Cost Reduction*. You have already revised your outline notes, to include both text and lecture ideas into one over-all outline.

You now turn that sheet of paper over and write across the top of the blank side: *The Five Roads to Cost Reduction – Test Questions*.

You are now ready to make up your questions. In do ing this you must remember that, in your final exam, you will be given two general types of questions.

First, the *Short-Answer* questions, such as multiplechoice, true-false, fill-in, and so on.

Second, the *Essay* questions, which ask you to write a paragraph or more in answer to every question.

In order to prepare for both types of questions, you draw a horizontal line across the middle of your paper, dividing it in two.

At the top left-hand comer of the upper half, right under the over-all title, write: *Short-Answer Questions:*

And at the top left-hand comer of the lower half, right under your dividing line, write: *Essay Questions:*

Now draw a vertical line down the middle of the paper, to divide your questions from your answers. Your paper now looks like this:

Five Roads to Cost Reduction — Test Questions

Short-Answer Questions   *Answers*

1.
2.
3.
4.
5.
6.
7.
8.

Essay Questions   *Answers*

1.

2.

3.

4.

5.

You are now ready to compose your questions.

HOW TO MAKE UP SHORT-ANSWER QUESTIONS

In Chapter 22, you will be shown each of the different types of short-answer questions, along with simple formulas to greatly aid you in answering them.

Here we can touch on only a few of these types of questions, to use as examples of how you should convert your lecture notes into a final self-quiz. You proceed in this way:

First, of course, you take every point that your teacher has emphasized in his lectures, and convert it into a test question.

Let's say, for example, that your teacher has stressed the methods of cutting capital equipment costs in his lecture. Immediately construct a cross-out test question on this point, and use it as the first short-answer question on the page, like this:

Which of the following four procedures is NOT a way to cut capital equipment costs?

> *a. Reducing costs of depreciation, replacement, maintenance, and interest.*
> *b. Holding down inventories.*
> *c. Operations research.*
> *d. Sharpening accounting procedures.*

The answer, of course, is c. But do not yet write in that answer. Instead, go on to the next question. This next series of questions revolves around those points that you have made errors on in previous work. For each error you have made, you now compose a self-test question.

For example, let's say you had difficulty before in remembering the various ways to cut raw-material costs. You now, therefore, construct a true-false question on just this point, in this way:

TRUE OR FALSE: Three good ways to cut raw material costs are precise purchasing specifications, inspection of incoming materials, and financial control of sources.

The answer, of course, is true. And so you go down the entire list of important points, constructing a different question for every one of the types mentioned in Chapter 22. In this way, you become thoroughly familiar with each one of these question types, *as they apply to the material you will be tested on.*

You even use the same procedure to make sure you know the exact meaning of each of the words in your fun damental vocabulary. For example, suppose you want to be absolutely certain of the meaning of *Operations Research*. To test yourself on this point, construct the following question:

OPERATIONS RESEARCH means most nearly: a) Cost Accounting; b) Statistical Decision Making; c) Computer Planning; d) Time and Motion Study.

The answer is c. But the construction of such a question forces you to think deeply about the meaning of this new word, to compare and contrast it with the other new terms you have learned in this course, and to dig deeper into more and more profitable levels of understanding.

HOW TO MAKE UP ESSAY QUESTIONS

The same procedure holds true on preparing your Essay Questions. First go over the important points stressed by your teacher. Then the points you have been confused on before. Then whatever other ideas you believe that you will be tested on in your final exam.

For each of these prepare an essay-type question, such as those described in Chapter 23.

For example, on manufacturing costs, a simple essay type question would be this:

List five ways to cut manufacturing costs.

Or, as a more complicated essay-type question:

You have just been appointed sales manager of the ABC Company. Describe five ways that you would attempt to cut their sales costs, in order, and tell why you think each of these ways would be effective.

HOW TO ANSWER ESSAY-TYPE QUESTIONS ON YOUR SELF-QUIZ PAPER

When you have written all your questions-both short answer and essay type-down the left-hand side of your paper, you are ready to take your own quiz and write the answers.

Do not do this the same day that you composed the questions. Wait a day, and then come back to the quiz. Without looking at your notes, write your answers. For the short-answer questions, write the answers completely. For the essay-type questions, however, do not write a complete answer. Instead, outline each of the answers as briefly as possible, and do not take the time to actually write in the outline as you would do in an actual test.

You are only trying to develop the main ideas for your answer; ·and the order in which you would arrange them. Once you have this, you can be satisfied, and go on to the next question.

For example, in the essay question two, about the sales manager position described on the last page, you should outline your answer in this way:

WAY TO CUT COST	REASON WHY
1. Advertising	*1. Biggest cost today*
2. Warehousing	*2. Greatest per-cent improvement*
3. Transportation	*3. Big waste in most co's.*
4. Direct Sales	*4. Fat usually creeps in*
5. New Specialists	*5. May be cut entirely*

HOW TO REVIEW YOUR SELF-QUIZZES

Once you have taken the test, you grade yourself right or wrong, just as your teacher would. Those answers that you have right you forget until the last day before the test.

Those answers that you have wrong you review again the next day, in this way:

Place a red check mark in frunt of the question you have missed. The next day, take out the self-quiz again, cover the answer with a sheet of fresh paper, and try to answer the question again.

If you get it correctly this second time, forget it until the last day before the test.

If you miss it again, reread your notes, and then turn back to the original textbook material and reread it again.

If you still do not understand it after this rereading immediately speak to your teacher about it, going over it with him until you are absolutely sure of it.

Remember your goal is to make certain that you understand every important idea in the course well enough to allow you to answer any question on it that can be thrown at you. You can accept nothing less.

WHAT THESE SELF-QUIZZES WILL DO FOR YOU

If you have done them correctly, when you are through with these self-quizzes, you have accomplished the dream of every person who has ever walked down a classroom aisle to take a final exam:

You will actually know the examination questions in advance!

You see, your teacher, in preparing his final tests, has no more material to choose from than you. Both you and your teacher will have to concentrate on the same broad ideas and important details as the sources for your test material.

Therefore, to a surprisingly large extent, you both must come up with exactly the same questions.

Think of the thrill you will get when you march into the final exam room and find dozens of the same exact test questions waiting there for you – *with the correct answers perfectly stored away in your head, ready to spring onto the paper.*

Think of the headstart this will give you over more poorly prepared classmates. Think of the tremendous burst of confidence this will raise in you – to completely erase any nervousness you might have brought into the room with you, to carry you right through every question on the test, with your mind already revved up to full working power, pulling out correct answers as fast as you can write them down on the page.

Isn't this a wonderful gift to give yourself, for only a few disciplined minutes each day, the final week before you take that test?

In summary:

A truly effective review is continuous self-examination of the essential parts of a course.

This continuous self-examination goes on every week of the course, right up until the final examination. It takes place in three stages:

1. *The weekly review.* Where you tie in every new chapter you have learned during the week with all the material that has gone before it. In this way you gain a constantly growing over-all view of the course, with all its important parts fresh in your mind.

2. *The final organization of your notebook.* Where you organize and blend in all the information you have received during the course – from your textbook, lectures, outside reference work, vocabulary building, and your error feed back. From this blending, you gain a final unified outline of the backbone ideas of the course, all at your fingertips for instant reference.

3. *The final quiz-review of the entire course.* Where you write your own final exam on the important ideas you have learned in the entire term, becoming familiar and at ease with both the content and form of such an exam. From this final self-quiz you gain dozens of the actual questions that will be asked of you in your final exam, plus the confidence that you can answer any other question that can be asked of you.

With this solid bedrock foundation of review to back you, we now turn to the final examinations themselves, and see dozens of simple ways to improve your performance in them.

CHAPTER 18

HIGH TECH WAYS TO
HACK THE LEARNING PROCESS

One thing you might have noticed is that so far, all of the methods outlined here are fairly low-tech. You can speed up your learning process without relying on technology – all you need is a pen, a notebook, and your brain.

However – and this is important – we don't live in the same world our grandparents lived in, or even our parents for that matter. Can you imagine… most of them did not even have cell phones when they were in school. We have technologies available to use that they never could have dreamed of. While it is important to master the basic techniques for reading information and retaining it, or for taking lecture notes, there is no reason why you can't then adapt and improve those techniques by utilizing technology.

This chapter is all about how to use technology to hack the learning process!

IDENTIFY HOW YOU LEARN BEST

The first step to using technology to hack the learning process is to look at how you learn best. By now you have some solid techniques to help you retain written and spoken information, but we are all unique – some of us learn better when information is presented in a certain way.

According to most experts, there are seven different ways of learning, but for the purposes of this chapter we are going to focus on the three kinds of learning that can the most easily adapted to technology:

• Aural
• Visual
• Verbal

If you are an aural learner, you learn things best by hearing them. Your brain absorbs information more quickly when you hear it spoken or played out loud. In addition to spoken words, other aural elements might also help you, such as music, rhymes, rhythms and other auditory cues.

If you are a visual learner, you learn things best by seeing them. You are far more likely to retain information transmitted to you in pictures, video, or even an infographic than you are to things that are written or spoken.

If you are a verbal learner, you learn things best by reading and writing them. You may even find that reading information out loud helps you to retain it better. Things like note taking and word games can really boost your ability to remember things you read.

Take a minute to think about times in your life when it's been easier for you to learn. Do you remember song lyrics very easily? You might be an aural learner. If you can watch something do it and remember how to do it yourself, you are most likely a visual learner. And finally, if you find it very easy to retain written information, you are probably a verbal learner.

Once you have identified the way you learn best, you can use technology to transform information you receive in one way into a format that will help you understand and retain it more easily.

HIGH TECH AURAL LEARNING

We've talked about active listening, and why it's important to identify the theme and main points of a lecture as soon as possible. What we haven't talked about yet is how human beings listen – the mechanics of it – and how the speed of human speech relates to the way we listen.

Most people speak at a rate of between 125 and 250 words per minute. That's a big range, but we all know at least one person who we'd describe as talking "a mile a minute." Chances are you don't have any person keeping up with your fast-talking friend when he gets going, right? The reason for that is that human beings can hear and retain information at a rate of about 400 words per minute!

That might seem like a big difference – and it is! – but it gets even more remarkable when you take into consideration the speed at which our brains can process information. We can think at a speed of about 1,000 to 3,000 words per minute. Whoa.

The difference between how fast people speak and how quickly you can listen and think creates something called a listening gap. Wouldn't it be cool if you could use technology to narrow that gap? Fortunately, you can.

For example, if you are an aural learner you might consider buying your textbooks in audio format – or ordering them on an e-reader that has text-to-voice capabilities. Many books in Kindle format have that option, and listening to them is probably a better option for aural learners.

Another way to hack aural learning is to record your lectures on a digital recorder and then save them as mp3 files. Once you do that, you can speed up the audio to listen at 2 times its speed – most apple devices will let you do that if you classic the file as an audiobook. By speeding up the recording, you can listen to an hour-long lecture in only 30 minutes!

HIGH TECH VISUAL LEARNING

What if you're a visual learner? You know that you will understand and retain information with less effort if you can see it rather than listening to it or reading it.

Just as it is possible to listen to audio files at twice their usual speed, you can watch videos the same way. If you are assigned to watch a video for class, you can use an app to let you play it back at twice its normal speed. One application that will do this (and speed up audio as well) is Swift Player or Azul for your mobile devices. You can speed up video direct from websites like YouTube, or download them to your computer. Another App that I use on my iPad is Quickreader. With it you can set the speed you want to read the book at and it goes through highlighting each line or sections of words for you using your preferred settings. This is great for reading books while you are on the treadmill or stationary bike – talk about doubling your productivity!

One thing you can do if you have to attend lectures but you are a visual learner, is to use your cell phone or a small digital camera to zoom in and record the lecture. Later, you can play it back at double the speed to enhance your absorption of new information.

Finally, you might consider doing things like printing photos or infographics and adding them to your written notes to help you remember more of what you learn. You can even use a website like Venngage to make your own infographics for free.

Another non-tech way to learn something twice as fast, if you are a visual learner, is to create mindmaps instead of just taking notes. Tony Buzan is the father of mindmapping and this is a very creative and visual way to take notes that also very effectively increases your learning and recall of the information. I won't go into any more detail on that since he literally wrote the book on the subject.

HIGH TECH VERBAL LEARNING

Finally, if you are a verbal learner there are several ways you can use technology to take information that is presented aurally or visually and get it into written form.

One thing I like to do is to use a LiveScribe pen to both take notes and record audio of a lecture. When you take notes, the notes are automatically transferred to your tablet or computer – plus the pen can record audio and sync it to your written notes. You can even use the mobile app to make the text you record searchable.

If you have to learn something that's been presented in video format, sometimes you have the option of viewing a transcript. But what do you do if there is no such option? There are a few apps you can use to do the same thing:

- Dragon Diction is a speech-to-text app that is available in the iTunes store. If you activate this app when you're in a lecture, it will automatically transcribe the lecture into written notes for you.
- Google Chrome has an add-on called Transcribe that will do the same thing. You can also use it to create written transcripts of videos and audio files.

These are only a few of the options available in terms of high-tech hacks based on different learning styles.

THE "TEACH SOMEONE ELSE" HACK

One of my favorite learning hacks is not high tech in and of itself – but you can combine it with the other techniques in this chapter to turn yourself into a learning powerhouse.

A study at Washington University in St. Louis showed that students who believed they would have to teach another student material they were studying performed better on subsequent tests than students who thought they were simply being tested on their own knowledge. There is something about knowing you will have to transmit information to others that helps you to break down knowledge you receive into its component parts.

Some ways to combine this technique with the high-tech methods we've discussed are:

- If you are a visual learner, take the information you've learned and make it into a graph, chart or infographic. Tell yourself that the graphic you create is going to be the only information another student will be given before they are tested on the material.

- If you are an aural learner, tell yourself that you have been asked to create a short podcast in order to convey the information you have earned to a group of students. Give yourself a time limit – for example, if you look at the chapters we analyzed earlier in the book, you would most likely need more time to teach the chapter about Greek history than you would to teach the chapter about sentence structure. Plan your time accordingly, and then – without planning out what you are going to say – record a five or ten minute podcast.

- If you are a verbal learner, assign yourself the task of writing a one or two page narrative of the information you have learned in your own words. Again, they key is to imagine that the words you write will be the ONLY information your hypothetical student gets to help them learn the material.

If you feel you must have an audience to make this work, ask a friend or family member to view your infographic, listen to your podcast, or read your summary. You could even play around with transferring your podcast to a written transcript or an infographic if the person you are teaching learns different than you do. There's a reason beginning writing students are sometimes told to write instructions on how to perform a certain task. When you are given the responsibility of relaying information to a third party, you approach your own learning in a different way.

The three suggestions above are meant to be a jumping-off point. If you can think of another, creative way to use technology to teach a real or hypothetical student about the subject you're studying, by all means – go for it! The point of this chapter is to show you that technology can be used to enhance your learning and make it even easier for you to retain information.

THE BOOK-SCANNING HACK

This next hack is one of my favorites, because it takes the basic reading and note-taking techniques described earlier in this book and uses technology to make them even more effective.

When we talked about reading, one of the things I told you to do was to pre-read each chapter to get a feeling for the overall structure, and then to underline or highlight key points in the text as you read. Following that advice can be the basis of some amazing high-tech hacks to help you get the most out of what you've read.

To do this hack, go ahead and do the following:

- Pre-read each chapter of the book to get an idea of the way it is put together and what it wants to teach you.

- Write out your questions so you know what information you're looking for.

- Read through everything aggressively and highlight anything that strikes you as important – anything that answers the questions you need to have answered.

- ALSO highlight chapter headings and relevant subheadings where you think it would help.

When you are done, you are going to take the entire book you've just read and scan it. The way I do this is to chop off the entire spine of the book and scan the individual pages – I have a Fuji ScanSnap scanner that will scan 50 pages at a time. This scanner also has OCR character-recognition capability.

Once I have scanned the entire book, I email the scanned pages off to my team and have them create a new document with only the highlighted text in it. When I get the new document back – usually we're talking about a 10 or 20 page document instead of a 200 or 300 page book – I immediately read it again.

My retention of the material I read this way is MORE THAN DOUBLED. Sure, it takes a little extra effort, but the end result is totally worth the time I spend doing the highlighting and scanning.

Now, if you're a student you might not have a team to take the text you highlight and turn it into a new document. No worries – there are a couple of different technologies you can use to bypass that step:

- Skim for Mac is an app that will let you extract highlights and notes from a PDF document (that's what most scanners will create) and put them into a new document.

- Sumnotes is a website that will do the same thing – you can paste your text in and it will extract what you specify, whether it is highlights, notes, or images. Not only that, but Sumnotes is a cloud-based technology, so you don't even have to install it on your computer. You can simply paste your text, and once you have the extracted information you can download it as a Word or Text document.

If you have an Amazon Kindle and have ordered books you need to read in Kindle format, there is another way you can use technology to hack your note taking.

When you read a book on a Kindle, you have the option to highlight text and to insert notes. For any book you read, you can go to the menu and ask to view your notes and highlights. If you do this, you can skip the scanning step altogether!

Highlighting text and making notes on a Kindle can be a bit slower than typing notes or highlighting with a marker, but the time you save scanning and scraping your notes into a separate document will even things out. You can even plug your Kindle into your PC, choose the "View my notes and highlights" option, and copy the notes and highlights into a separate document for printing or re-reading.

The one area where this can be tricky with a Kindle is that the highlights and notes option doesn't work as well for personal document as it does for books you buy from the Kindle store. However, there is an app you can use that can help. It's called ezPDF Reader, and you can find it in the Amazon store. It's also available for Android.

The ezPDF Reader is worth getting if you have a Kindle. The built-in PDF reader on Kindles is not great, but this app allows you to upload PDF files, annotate them in a number of different ways, and then export your notes in various file formats. It also has a very functional voice option that will read documents to you if you prefer – so basically, it gives you the ability to turn any personal document into an audio book!

As you can see, the learning hacks in this book are extremely versatile. Once you understand your ideal learning style, you can couple the basic reading and note-taking techniques you've learned with all kinds of cool technologies to super-charge your learning process. Once you get used to learning this way, you will never look back.

EPILOGUE

HOW TO MAKE YOURSELF INTO A MENTAL CHAMPION

There it is. You now have the techniques you need to learn anything in half the time.

They are simple, fast, and enormously effective. Used properly, they can get you the job you might have missed, the recognition and prestige that may have passed you by, the extra pay raises that might have otherwise slipped through your fingers – *all the rewards in life that go only to the well-prepared, well-educated person who can use every drop of power of his brain is capable of.*

But they can't do a darned one of these things without your active support!

Reading these techniques--even learning them-is just not enough. Teaching them to yourself is not enough. Even memorizing them is not enough.

They are no good to you until they become SECOND NATURE! Until they are built into your nervous system as reaction patterns or habits. Until you do them automatically, perfectly, without thinking. As easily and quickly and naturally as you now write your name.
And this means PRACTICE!
PRACTICE!
PRACTICE!

Champions in any field, whether it be art, or sports, or business, or study, are made by two great tools:

1. Knowledge or technique.

2 . Practice to perfect that technique.

The first element, knowledge, can be bought. It can be bought in the form of a book, or a lecture, or even in the form of hard experience.

But the second element, practice, can only be earned. It is a function of character. It is a result of that inner drive, persistence, endurance, patience, will to win, inability to quit that makes the champion.

In life, it is not intelligence that makes the greatest difference. We have all seen too many brilliant minds left panting behind – shattered and defeated – doomed to lives of nameless mediocrity.

In life, ultimately, *it is drive that counts!* The tortoise still wins; the hare still is left sleeping in obscurity!

"A winner never quits; a quitter never wins!"

"Practice makes perfect."

This is old wisdom. True wisdom. Wisdom that works today in the science laboratory as much as it did in the groves of Socratic Greece.

Teach it to yourself. Build into your brain, not only the techniques that produce sucecss, but the drive that will settle for nothing less than success, and you will have learned the most powerful secret of success in the entire world! A secret that will open up an entire new world of accomplishment to you!

Good luck! And good learning!

www.ingramcontent.com/pod-product-compliance
Lightning Source LLC
Chambersburg PA
CBHW071756090426
42737CB00012B/1841